Solving
Your Child's
Behavior Problems

Solving
Your Child's
Behavior Problems

By Dr. Jeffrey Kelly

Little, Brown and Company
Boston / Toronto / London

FIRST EDITION

Library of Congress Cataloging in Publication Data

Kelly, Jeffrey A.
  Solving your child's behavior problems.

  Bibliography: p.
  Includes index.
  1. Behavior therapy.   2. Problem children.
3. Child rearing.   I. Title.
RJ505.B4K44   1983   649'.64   82-24928
ISBN 0-316-48696-5
ISBN 0-316-48695-7 (pbk.)

10 9 8 7 6 5 4 3 2

BP

Designed by Dede Cummings

*Published simultaneously in Canada
by Little, Brown & Company (Canada) Limited*

PRINTED IN THE UNITED STATES OF AMERICA

*To my own Mother and Father, and to
Debbie, Irene, and Mario*

Acknowledgments

MANY people have contributed to the development of this book in both direct and indirect ways. My colleagues at the University of Mississippi Medical Center, and especially the psychology residents with whom I work in our Child Clinic, have helped to refine and put into practice many of the approaches described in this book. Ron Drabman, as a supervisor and then as a colleague, influenced my own style of treating families and children. And, perhaps more than all others, I owe a debt of gratitude to the families who have come to our clinic. From them we have learned.

Janet St. Lawrence, Drew Bradlyn, Karen Christoff, Dan Franco, and Bill Himadi are psychologists who offered very helpful comments and suggestions on each chapter's content; without their help, it would have been much more difficult to write this book. Allen Hauth, as he has always done, gave me much encouragement along the way. Wauline Carter's skilled secretarial assistance was invaluable throughout the book's preparation. Linda Nelson and Deborah Jurkowitz provided not only their special expertise but also their support. And, finally, a special thanks to the Krystal Number Four, where most of this book was written.

Contents

Introduction

"My four-year-old boy is afraid of the dark and doesn't want to sleep alone. What can I do about it?"

"Chuck is five years old but still has a problem with bed-wetting. It's bothering him, and frankly, it's bothering us, too. The pediatrician says the problem isn't physical, but we're not sure how to help Chuck overcome the bed-wetting."

"I hate to spank my child for misbehaving. Are there other ways to discipline misbehavior?"

"What's the best way to handle a child's temper tantrums?"

"I want my daughter to grow up able to think for herself and to make decisions independently. Is there a way to help a five-year-old start to do this?"

"Susan is very, very shy. I know there's nothing wrong with being a little shy, but it concerns me that she has such trouble making friends. Can I help her to become more outgoing?"

"Mark and James always fight, even though they're brothers. I'd like them to learn to work out their disagreements without attacking each other, but I haven't been able to get them to do this."

"I'm going back to work and Tina, who is three, will need to go to day-care while I'm working. There are a lot of day-care and preschool programs where I live, but I want to pick the very best one. What should I look for?"

RAISING children *is* a challenge. It's also one of the most important, time-consuming, demanding, but potentially gratifying tasks that people can ever encounter.

For most of the important jobs in our lives, we receive long and intensive preparation. To prepare us for good citizenship, high schools and colleges provide courses in civics, history, and current affairs. To prepare us for work, we take background courses in school that are followed by specialized training in whatever kind of employment we plan to pursue. We even learn, through school and other structured experiences, such things as how to stay physically healthy, how to be a wise consumer, and how to keep our personal finances straight.

Yet in the even more important task of raising children, people usually have very little experience or preparation to guide them. For the most part, we have to fall back on three basic but imperfect strategies for learning how to raise our children. The first and most important influence is the experience of our own upbringing. People tend to raise their children in much the same way that they themselves were raised. Intentionally or not, we imitate the values, disciplinary style, strengths, and limitations shown by our own parents.

Second, parents make decisions based on their own judgment. For example, when a child misbehaves, parents usually rely on judgment to tell them whether to ignore the misbehavior, have a heart-to-heart discussion with the child, scold, spank, or use some other form of discipline.

Third, we learn to parent by sheer trial and error. Especially with a first child, when parents encounter a situation they don't know how to handle, they often simply guess about what to do and hope it turns out right. Later children are usually raised with a bit less guesswork (and a lot less anxiety on the parents' part) since the parent has already had the experience of raising a child before them.

In many situations, these three things — doing what our own parents did, using our best judgment, and even trial and error — are sufficient to guide parents in the task of raising their children. That, after all, is how most of us were raised. But this informal approach doesn't work all the time. Each child is unique and exhibits different kinds of behavior problems as well as different strengths and abilities. The examples and questions at the beginning of this section reflect just some of the problems commonly faced by parents of children from three to six years old. They are also the questions that parents ask child psychologists, including the professionals at our own child clinic. Today, as a result of psychologists' better understanding of children and their behavior, it is possible to provide practical and specific advice on how parents can solve many of the everyday behavior problems encountered by young children.

"Be permissive and tolerant!"

"Be strict and firm!"

"Communicate openly with your child!"

"Don't be afraid to discipline!"

Parents get a lot of different and often contradictory advice about the kinds of parents they should be. Our purpose isn't to convince you to become a certain kind of parent, but to present some down-to-earth strategies for handling your child's behavior problems. Our approach for solving behavior problems is based on the principles of behavior therapy, an approach that stresses that people (including children) learn to behave in certain ways as a result of their experiences and the consequences of their actions. Parents are in a position to help their children learn good patterns of behavior, learn important new living skills, and learn to think positively about themselves. This book will offer you guidance in how to solve problems and promote this growth process.

The approaches we present have been shown to be effective not only in many different child clinics (including our own) but also in detailed research studies of children's behavior problems. It's our hope that this book will be of help to you, too.

Solving
Your Child's
Behavior Problems

1/
Why Children Misbehave

YOU love your child, and like most parents, you want your child to grow up to be happy and successful. You also know that with the exception of some families on television shows — the families that never seem to have any problems with their kids and in which no one apparently even has to work — the real-world practice of raising children is a good deal more complex. Your child misbehaves and you are not sure how to handle the behavior problems that are starting to concern (and occasionally to anger or frustrate) you.

The focus of this book is on solving behavior problems of children from three to six years old. This certainly does not mean that parents never encounter difficulties with their children before this age range: infants and early toddlers can also present real challenges in parenting. However, the ages of three to six are special in several ways. As children approach three, there is an exceptionally rapid development of new skills and competencies: language, speech, and vocabulary all become more complex; the capacity to think and reason begins to take form; children become much more active and curious about their environment; and they begin to develop playmates. The person we looked upon before as an infant or a toddler is now becoming a child with behaviors distinctly his own.

As children change, grow, and start to behave in new ways, parents need to develop new strategies for interacting with them. Usually, this means helping your child learn new skills.

For children in the younger range of our three-to-six age period, many of the developmental skills that need to be mastered involve self-control and delaying gratification. At this stage parents often need to help their children become fully toilet trained, learn not to bed-wet, and to be able to convey their wishes in ways other than tantrums.

As children become a bit older, they also become much more independent in their play and social activities with others and are able to think more elaborately about things that happen to them. With these new developments come additional tasks for the child and, from time to time, problems. As a four-year-old becomes more purposeful and intent in his daily activities, he may also become more frustrated and angry when things don't go the way he likes. This requires learning to express feelings appropriately, rather than through temper outbursts, noncompliance, or destructiveness. As a five-year-old spends more time away from the security of her home, she may encounter things that are frightening and unfamiliar. Learning to overcome fears and gain self-confidence are important tasks at this point. At about the same age, children are able to assume greater responsibility for making everyday decisions about matters that affect them. Finally, as they approach the age of six, youngsters tend to be much more involved with playmates and friends, and they will soon be starting school. At this point, new social skills and friend-making behavior become important.

While there are predictable milestones in most children's development — for example, youngsters start walking by their first birthday, are usually ready for toilet training by two, and most begin formal kindergarten at the age of five — it isn't always possible to chronologically pinpoint either the mastery of specific tasks or the behavior problems that may be encountered. For that reason, this book stresses the kinds of behavior problems that most commonly occur during these early years and the ways that parents can handle problems whenever they develop. The appendix located at the end of the book summarizes some common childhood behavior problems and discusses the ages at which they are often encountered.

Given the many new tasks faced by all children during this early period of their lives, difficulties in handling these new responsibilities — what we term "behavior problems" — will occasionally occur. How do they develop and at what point do behavior problems become serious enough to merit a parent's concerned attention?

SEARCHING FOR THE CAUSES OF BEHAVIOR PROBLEMS

Over the years, professionals have attempted to locate the causes of personality in general, and behavior disorders in particular, by looking in some unlikely places. Centuries ago, personality style was thought to be caused by liquids or "humors" that flowed through the circulatory system of the body. When an excess of one kind of liquid predominated, it might account for a person's irritability, listlessness, depression, or overactivity. Some years later, professionals become equally and enthusiastically convinced that the shape, size, and contour of an individual's head could predict his or her behavior. Calling the science "phrenology" and equipped with tape measures and calipers, early physicians dutifully measured the heads of their young patients to locate the bumps responsible for maladaptive behavior. As recently as the early part of this century, professionals had become convinced that personality characteristics were related to physical build and stature. People with a high proportion of body fat were presumed to be given to mood swings, thin persons to be introverted and shy, and athletic types to be outgoing and stable.

All of these attempts to understand the development of children's personality have long since been disproven, but we continue to try to locate the causes (and solutions) to children's behavior problems in some equally unlikely places. Several widely accepted assumptions about children's behavior problems that turn out *not* to be so true include these:

If children often act like their parents, does this mean they inherited personality characteristics from them? We know that children do inherit many physical characteristics: such attributes as eye color, hair color, and height are genetically determined. Although the theory is somewhat controversial, many psychologists now believe that the intelligence of a child is substantially determined by genetic factors. But we also know that children do tend to behave the way their parents do. For example, high-strung parents tend to have emotional children, achievement-oriented parents tend to have children who set high standards for their own performance, introverted parents are more likely to have shy children, and so on. This leads some people to assume that all of these behavioral characteristics must therefore be inherited as well. Actually, most current studies have failed to show any clear genetic link between the personalities of parents and the personalities of their children. When children behave as others in their family do, it is because they have learned to behave this way, either by observing and copying the actions of other family members or because parents are likely to reward characteristics in their children that they themselves exhibit. There is little evidence to suggest that behavioral personality characteristics are caused by genetic or hereditary factors.

Aren't behavior problems the symptoms of some deeper emotional condition that cannot be treated directly? At one time this was the dominant theory in the field of child study. The notion was that a child's misbehaviors (whether they involve fighting, tantrumming, problems in toilet training, or being afraid of the dark) were caused by events, conflicts, or an emotional trauma hidden somewhere in the past, usually carried over from infancy or very early childhood. Thus, behavior problems were viewed only as outward symptoms which neither could nor should be treated directly since they were being caused by something deeper.

However, there were some serious challenges to the idea that children's behavior problems are caused by deep-seated emotional turmoil from the past. One was the simple lack of evidence that the vast majority of children who misbehave ever experienced any unusual emotional trauma at a critical stage of early development. While it is true that a child who undergoes a major, devastating upset (such as extreme neglect or parental abuse) in early life may well experience problems later, most children who exhibit behavior problems have not had such experiences. And from a practical point of view, even if they have, the parent will still need to learn to handle the child's current actions, regardless of their cause. The psychological treatment literature of the past ten years shows quite clearly that children's behavior problems not only can but also should be dealt with directly.

The brain ultimately controls all behavior. Therefore, aren't behavior problems often the result of brain malfunction? The first part of this statement is absolutely correct. All human behavior — moving, thinking, talking, sensing, breathing — is governed by the brain and central nervous system. Without the nervous system functioning reasonably well there would be no life, let alone behavior problems. This fact has led to speculation that many childhood behavior disorders might themselves be traceable to brain abnormalities. In particular the notion of "minimal brain dysfunction" has enjoyed a good deal of recent attention from segments of the professional community. This theory speculates that tiny (and often clinically undetectable) brain abnormalities are responsible for various kinds of mis-behaviors. The behavior problems most often linked to supposed brain dysfunction include overactivity, learning and school problems, aggression, and tantrumming.

Like many theories, this one contains at least an element of accuracy. Some children do have nervous system disorders or brain damage that can be objectively diagnosed by neurologists using EEGs and similar medical brain activity tests, as well as by psychologists using specialized brain function assessments. And there are specific consequences of those nervous system abnormalities, including epilepsy and related seizure disorders as well as certain perceptual processing disorders known as learning disabilities. But unless there is clear medical evidence of such a disorder, parents can assume that their children's ordinary behavior problems are not caused by brain abnormalities, even when those behavior problems have been severe and longstanding.

Isn't a child's personality "fixed" by the age of five? Perhaps the easiest way to correct this assumption is simply to think about yourself. Do you act now the way you did when you were five years old? Of course not. You've developed different interests, competencies, fears, ways of handling relationships, and ways of thinking. All of those characteristics we call personality change over time. Experiences throughout childhood, adolescence, adulthood, and older age change us, and the development of what we call our personality is a continuing process, not a pattern that somehow becomes arrested at a certain age. However, it is important to recognize that both positive and negative events occurring in childhood may have a greater impact than events that occur later in life, because children have a reduced range of life experiences. Making one's first close friend (or losing one's first close friend) has a greater impact on a child because his or her experience of having friends is still relatively limited. Similarly, early learning experiences affect a child's behavior more profoundly than they would an adult. Because it is possible to alter behavior more easily in childhood than in adulthood, solving the behavior problems of children is easier than solving those same behavior problems if they persist into adolescence and adult life.

Do behavior problems reflect a stage that a child is passing through? Will they solve themselves in time? Do problem behaviors appear and then disappear without any particular attention from parents? This is an important question since, if misbehaviors are spontaneously outgrown, the major job of parents would simply be waiting out the problems until they disappear.

Some problems will go away, but others are not easily resolved and can persist or even worsen as time goes by. Children who have severe fears (such as extreme fear of the dark, fear of animals, or fear of strangers) may have them for a relatively long period of time. The reason for this is that anyone's natural response is to stay away from things that frighten them. Kids who are afraid of the dark will sleep in bright rooms, kids who fear animals will go to great lengths to avoid any contact with them, and so on. However, a problem then arises because, by avoiding contact with what we fear, we lose the opportunity to overcome that fear. Children can't find out firsthand that what they were afraid of really isn't so frightening unless they can be gradually exposed to it.

The same kind of problem carryover tends to occur for children who have difficulties interacting with others. Studies that have followed isolated, shy, and friendless children through their later life show that these persons tend to have more adjustment and social problems as adults. If a child lacks the skills that are needed to make friends early in life, the child will develop fewer friends, be more isolated, and have correspondingly fewer opportunities to develop close relationships as he grows older as well. Aggressive behavior problems also tend to persist, in part because aggressiveness often gets children what they want from others.

While some misbehaviors are temporary in nature and seem to disappear almost as rapidly as they developed, others become more habitual and may even worsen over time. Whenever children's problem behaviors become a source of conflict within a family, whenever they are sufficient to cause the child unhappiness or frustrate the parents' attempts to solve them, then it becomes time for the parents to develop systematic new ways to deal with their children more effectively. Waiting to see whether certain problems will be outgrown naturally is a luxury that children with behavior problems (and their parents) often cannot afford.

HOW DO BEHAVIOR PROBLEMS USUALLY DEVELOP?

If the behavior problems of children are not inherited, aren't being caused by some underlying emotional conflict, and are not the result of some nervous system or brain disorder, where *do* they come from? In almost all instances, children's behavior problems are *learned*. This strikes most parents as surprising, since no well-intentioned parent ever seeks to teach a child to misbehave and most parents actively try to teach their children good behavior. Part of the difficulty involves what we mean by "learning." Generally, people think of learning as a formal educational process, the kind followed by parents or teachers when they want to give children some new knowledge. But another kind of learning is much less formal, structured, and planned. This is the learning of behavior patterns based on the consequences of one's actions, and it is this form of learning — learning from experience — that is most responsible for the development of behavior patterns.

A THREE-STEP PROCESS FOR SOLVING YOUR CHILD'S BEHAVIOR PROBLEMS

Parents are in the unique position of being able to directly help their children develop more appropriate, successful, and positive patterns of behavior. This is because parents can create powerful consequences for their children's actions, consequences that can foster the learning of desirable personal characteristics and solve existing behavior problems. As a parent, you are in a position to strengthen or reinforce positive qualities and behaviors such as self-control, following reasonable directions, or playing cooperatively with others. You are also in a position to arrange learning experiences that will reduce your child's negative behavior problems, including such misbehaviors as tantrums, dawdling, fighting with others, destructiveness, and noncompliance. Finally, the principles of learning from experience can be used to teach your child new skills and competencies such as toilet training, overcoming shyness and fears, and making decisions.

But merely being in the position to solve your child's behavior problems is not enough. Several steps must be followed to change children's actions. The *first step* is to become familiar with those learning principles that guide the process of child behavior change. The *second step* is to develop a plan to apply these principles to your child's unique behavior problems. The *third and most important step* is to carry out that plan with your child. Over the past six years we have used this kind of three-step procedure for solving children's behavior problems at our medical center's child psychology treatment clinic. The process has been used successfully with hundreds of families and with dozens of different kinds of behavior problems. It is an approach suitable for parents whose children are exhibiting mild behavior problems as well as for those whose children exhibit longstanding problems that have proven difficult to manage and change.

In the next three chapters we will review the basic learning principles that you as a parent will need to understand in order to bring about positive change in your child's behavior. The principles cover ways to increase good behavior and decrease misbehavior, and they demonstrate how children learn by watching others. It is these principles which form the foundation for the specific techniques we will discuss later. By becoming familiar with the general methods of child behavior change, you will be in a position not only to handle the problems that we specifically discuss, but also to handle new problems that might develop in the future. The remainder of the book describes the most common behavior problems children encounter and tells step by step how you as a parent can handle them successfully.

The procedures described here are straightforward, practical, and common sense. Too often, parents have asked direct questions about how they should handle their child's behavior problems but have been given only vague answers by professionals. Because it is the parent who spends the greatest amount of time with his or her child, it is the parent who is in a good position to improve the child's behavior, so long as practical and specific information on what to do is being provided. This system does just that.

Improvement in child behavior (and family interactions) often occurs quickly. When parents first become concerned with — and later frustrated by — behavior problems that don't seem to go away, their interactions with their children may become increasingly negative and characterized by ineffective scolding, nagging, threatened spankings, and the like. This is unfortunate but understandable. As parents actually learn to change the way troublesome situations are handled, corresponding improvement in children's behavior often occurs fairly quickly. This is because the parents are intentionally and systematically creating a new family learning environment conducive to the development of more positive child behavior. How quickly improvement comes about depends largely on the diligence and consistency with which parents handle misbehaviors, but visible improvement within several weeks is the rule, rather than the exception, for most of the behavior problems we will discuss.

Child behavior change is accomplished largely through positive techniques rather than punishment. As we will see, it is necessary to punish certain child misbehaviors, and occasionally it is necessary to spank. We'll discuss how and when to do this. More often than most people realize, however, children's misbehaviors can be dealt with effectively (and more pleasantly for both the parent and the child) through reward-based systems. This means that you can not only solve the child's behavior problems, but you can do so in a way that actually enhances the quality of your relationship with your child. Let's see how.

2/

Strengthening Your Child's Good Behavior Patterns

TO understand why children do the things they do, or more important, to understand why they sometimes don't do what we want them to do, we need to know a little about human motivation in general. Once we become familiar with some of the principles that account for people's actions, we can apply those principles to solve certain behavior problems that children have.

Let's begin by imagining that someone from another planet is deposited one day on Earth. The visitor's job is to observe how people spend their time, in order to better understand human civilization and habits. In all probability, our observer would see things that seem rather strange and difficult to explain. He would see large, sprawling buildings called high schools with rooms full of people who sit all day long at desks. Why do people sit in these dull-looking places all day when it is clear that most of them would really rather be doing other things with their time, things like going to the beach, playing baseball, or spending time with friends?

The alien would see other buildings with slightly older people in them, again spending all day long at their desks. These places, that humans refer to as "work" or "the office," also seem like strange locations for people to spend so much time in. What makes them do it? What makes people leave their homes every morning and head to work when they, too, would probably prefer to do things other than working in offices all day?

Then our observer sees something even more baffling. He watches two humans who seem to spend a great deal of their time together. The man and woman he is watching smile at one another, exchange affectionate glances, eat lunch together, and walk down the street holding hands. Before they separate, they kiss and say how much they are looking forward to seeing a movie together that night. It is apparent that these two humans want to be with each other, and the alien again wonders why people do this. Why it is that people want to be together as couples, to be with each other so much?

What is puzzling to this visitor from outer space — and it's a matter that most of us rarely think about — involves our motivation for doing the things we do. After all, spending the entire day at school or at work seems not to be what most people would automatically do on their own. They certainly aren't things people would do every day without some good reasons. If we ask someone to tell us why he or she goes to work every day, the person is likely to think for a while and then give reasons like these:

"I work to make money so I can pay my bills and do things I enjoy."

"I enjoy hearing from others and knowing myself that I do a good job."

"I like the prestige and status of my job."

"I get satisfaction from the job's challenges."

"I like the people I work with."

"It's more interesting for me to be at work than to spend all day just sitting at home."

"I see my job as an avenue that will lead to other jobs I'd like to have in the future."

When people provide reasons like these to account for their actions, they are really identifying rewards or *reinforcers* that account for what they do. In this example, the person is saying that he works every day because working leads to rewarding or reinforcing consequences of various kinds. Some of the reinforcers this person mentioned are fairly basic, such as receiving a salary. Others are more internalized, such as being able to tell yourself you did a good job, feeling satisfaction, and experiencing a sense of accomplishment. But the important point here is that all of us learn to do things that lead to reinforcing and positive consequences. If you don't think this is true, imagine how long you would keep working if your boss one day said that you would henceforth do only things you hate, that you would never be told that you'd done anything well, and that you'd no longer be paid.

We can analyze many of our other activities in this way. If you think of things you habitually do — whether they involve school, work, hobbies, or even your relationships with others — you will probably find that there are rewards or reinforcers of some kind that account for your behavior. To the extent that an activity leads to these gratifications, you'll keep doing it. To the degree that rewards for your behavior cease to be forthcoming, you will most likely become dissatisfied and stop that activity. People drop out of school, quit jobs, change jobs, even end social relationships if these activities are no longer reinforcing.

This same important principle applies to the behavior of children. Stated simply, children learn to do things that lead to positive consequences for them and they learn to avoid engaging in activities that don't. This principle of reinforcement tells us that the best way to motivate a child's good behavior — to get a child to do things he or she now doesn't do — is by developing a plan to reinforce or reward the good actions we want to see.

WHAT KINDS OF REINFORCERS MOTIVATE BEHAVIOR?

We can think of reinforcers as rewards or gratifications that fall within three levels of complexity. The most basic kind of reinforcer is the *tangible* or *concrete reward*. A tangible reward is an identifiable, concrete object or privilege. Among adults, tangible rewards include salaries or money, a new car, going to a favorite restaurant, and playing a sport that one enjoys. Children also respond to (and will work to earn) tangible incentives. Parents sometimes provide their children with spending allowances in exchange for willingness to complete chores or similar responsibilities. Here the allowance functions as a reinforcer that motivates the child to assume more grown-up responsibilities. Staying up late, an ice cream cone, a special trip to a park, and watching a television show are still other examples of concrete or tangible rewards.

The next higher level of reinforcer is *attention or praise* from others. With very few exceptions, people greatly enjoy positive recognition for their accomplishments. Hearing a heartfelt "You did a good job," "I'm very proud of you," or "That was great!" from people we know tells us that they noticed our actions and it leads us to work harder to continue to get that recognition. The best teachers and the best bosses, for example, tend to be people who routinely motivate others by noticing and commenting on their accomplishments. The worst teachers or bosses (and most of us have known some firsthand) are those who comment only when a problem develops and appear to ignore an individual's day-to-day successes. Praise and attention are powerful incentives for children, too. Just as adults respond and work hard to earn positive recognition from others who matter to them, children do the same thing. As kids learn that they *will* get noticed and praised when they behave well, their good behavior patterns become strengthened. As we will see shortly, one of the most critical tasks for parents is to learn how to use their attention and praise to motivate a child's good actions, especially those good actions that don't happen often enough now.

A third and still higher level of reinforcement that affects our behavior is the ability to reward ourselves. *Self-reinforcement* takes place when we are able to recognize our own accomplishments, to realize that we've done something well, and to take pride in our own conduct. Most adults live in a world where they don't get tangible rewards, notice, and attention from others every time they do something significant. Yet even when these outside reinforcers are not present, people can compliment themselves internally. "I really worked hard on that report," "I did a good job there," or "It's good to help other people" are rewarding things we tell ourselves to guide and motivate our actions even when no one else notices what we did. Someone who does kind things for others with no visible benefit to himself, such as the individual who anonymously donates large gifts to the needy, is probably responding not to any external gratification but to the positive feeling he derives from being charitable.

These three kinds of reinforcers, taken together, account for many of the things people do. Why, in a book about solving children's behavior problems, should we be so concerned about the motivation of adults? Because the motivations for adult behavior are not fundamentally different from those that guide our children's behavior. We need to remember that just as adults become disinterested, neglectful, and stop engaging in activities that do not lead to gratification and positive outcomes of some kind, children often fail to behave well when their good behavior isn't being sufficiently reinforced.

USE ATTENTION AND PRAISE TO STRENGTHEN YOUR CHILD'S GOOD BEHAVIOR

An old adage says that it's the squeaky wheel that gets the grease, meaning that we tend to notice something when it is going badly and not when it is going well. Children also tend to get noticed most when they are misbehaving rather than when they are behaving well. Too often, parents make the mistake of taking a child's good behavior for granted and forget to direct attention and approval to the youngster when he is behaving appropriately. Because attention and notice from a parent are reinforcers to most children, kids will do the things that elicit this attention. If children learn that they can get noticed by misbehaving, they will misbehave more often. But if they learn that good behavior is what gains recognition from their parents, children will become motivated to earn that approval through their good actions.

Mrs. Parker's four-year-old son Todd is causing problems. Although he has plenty of toys and games to play with, he quickly loses interest in them and seeks out other things to do. In the past week alone he has colored with crayons on three different walls, pulled dishes off the table, and tried "playing" with the family dog by chasing it with a stick.

Mrs. Parker explained that she lets Todd play by himself but when she senses that he is about to misbehave, she tries to keep a closer eye on him. When Todd leaves his toys and starts crayoning on the wall or chasing the dog, she immediately scolds him. Mrs. Parker is almost beginning to get the feeling that Todd does some of these things to aggravate her.

In this example, the parent wanted her child to play with his toys to entertain himself, rather than play in unacceptable ways. That's reasonable. But if we look more closely at what the mother is actually doing here, we can see that she provides very little notice when Todd behaves well, and gives her attention (in this case, coming over to Todd and scolding) primarily when he's acting badly. Without knowing it, the parent is really reinforcing the child's misbehavior!

Our advice to Mrs. Parker was not complicated. Bearing in mind that attention is a reinforcer, the solution to this problem was to get the parent to provide that attention to Todd when he played appropriately and not when he misbehaved. Whenever Todd started playing with one of his toys, Mom came over and told him she was happy to see him play so well. Periodically while Todd played, she would ask him to explain what he was building with his blocks or she would take a few minutes to join in his games. All of this showed Todd that his mother was interested in his activities and that she approved of his appropriate play. Mrs. Parker was now providing her attention when Todd behaved well, and thereby strengthening that good behavior pattern.

While Todd did start playing with his toys more, there were still times when he would turn to more destructive play habits. As soon as Mrs. Parker saw Todd about to misbehave, we asked her to stop him quickly and without fuss explain in just a sentence or two why he shouldn't engage in the bad activity ("Todd, I don't want you to tease the dog. It's not fair to do that to him"), and then direct the child back to an appropriate play activity. As soon as Todd started to play well, Mrs. Parker resumed praising and recognizing his desirable actions. This strengthened them even more.

You may find yourself wondering why Mrs. Parker's earlier scoldings were actually reinforcing Todd's bad behavior. After all, scolding may be attention, but it doesn't sound like a rewarding kind of attention. One might think that scolding would lessen bad incidents. For children who are very rarely scolded, this approach sometimes does work. But when children are scolded often for misbehaving, they simply get used to it. Scolding becomes merely another form of attention. That's why it's so important to turn this pattern around: if you want your youngster to do something more often, *provide plenty of praise and attention while the youngster is behaving well.* As much as you possibly can, develop the strategy of praising your child's good actions rather than scolding the youngster when he or she is not behaving well.

THE KEYS TO USING PRAISE EFFECTIVELY:
BE CONSISTENT, BE SPECIFIC, AND BE GENUINE

Even when parents understand that their attention can motivate a child's good behavior, they still may not be using that attention in the most effective way.

Melissa always leaves things a mess. When she changes her clothes, the dirty ones end up scattered across the floor of her bedroom. When she plays, her toys are left all over the room. When she takes things out of her bureau, she never remembers to put them back. Melissa's mother isn't a cleanliness fanatic, but she does think it would be nice if her five-year-old child took a bit more responsibility for herself in this way.

The parent has tried several times to praise Melissa for picking up after herself. But after a day or two she fell back into the routine of nagging the child and now just gathers up her daughter's clothes and toys herself several times a day rather than argue with the child about it.

In order to use praise and attention to improve your child's conduct, you should keep in mind several points about how children learn. The first is that kids learn new patterns of behavior best when they are consistently reinforced for those new actions, when they receive at least some recognition every time the desired action occurs. This means that it isn't enough to occasionally praise your child for doing something he or she doesn't usually want to do. If Melissa never picks up her toys or clothes, it will require a lot of consistent recognition from her parents in order to firmly change this bad-behavior pattern. When the parent praises the child for picking things up some of the time, but then pays no attention on other occasions when the child does this, and at still other times nags Melissa, the connection between the youngster's desirable behavior (being neat) and the reward (attention or praise) that can strengthen it is inconsistent. The rule for parents, then, is to notice every time that your child behaves well in what had been the problem area and to let your child know you are pleased.

A second aspect of praise that makes it more effective is letting your youngster know exactly what he is doing that pleases you. Melissa's mother might notice her daughter putting her dirty clothes in the hamper one afternoon and tell the child

"That's good." But it is much better to let a youngster also know the reason you are happy with her improved conduct. Rather than a general "That's good," the parent might instead say "Melissa, I'm happy that you're putting away those dirty clothes. You're like a big girl helping her mother when you do that." This helps any child realize not only that the parent noticed the good behavior, but also conveys exactly what action was so pleasing to the parent.

Finally, it is important to recognize that using praise and attention to improve your child's actions works only to the degree that your child realizes that you are genuinely pleased. If your youngster does something you want to see him do more often, convey your recognition of the good behavior in a warm, sincere, and demonstrative way. While most parents have little difficulty genuinely venting their anger, frustration, or irritation when a child misbehaves, the far more important skill for parents to develop is being able to clearly express their positive feelings when the child behaves well.

USE ENJOYABLE ACTIVITIES OR PRIVILIGES TO REWARD CHILDREN

You can probably recall times when you have had some necessary, but not especially pleasant, task to accomplish. The task might have been doing housework, cutting the lawn, working on a report for work or school, or some other thing that you really didn't want to do but felt you needed to do. A strategy people often use to get motivated at such times is allowing themselves to do something fun, but only when they have first completed the activity that isn't so much fun. "When I finish the report I'll relax and watch television," "As soon as I do this housework I'll sit down, have a cup of tea, and read my magazine," or "I'll go play golf once this grass gets cut" are all examples of the deals we strike with ourselves to accomplish jobs we might otherwise avoid or put off. You can probably identify other examples of this self-motivation approach that you yourself use.

Whenever we allow ourselves to do something enjoyable in return for first doing something necessary but not so much fun, we are really applying the reinforcement principle to our own behavior. In this case, the rewarding activity (relaxing, watching TV, playing golf, whatever) becomes a reinforcer that increases our willingness to do the less pleasant task. This self-reward motivation system works, of course, only if we are really prepared to follow through on the self-made deal or contract: if the grass doesn't get cut, there won't be a golf game, or if the report isn't written, I won't allow myself to watch that favorite TV show. In this way, getting the reward depends on doing the less pleasant task first.

Using an enjoyable activity as a reward for following through on less enjoyable tasks is a system that also works very well with children, and it's an especially effective way for encouraging children to accept responsibilities that they presently avoid. In Melissa's case, the parent could have taken just this approach to solving her child's behavior problem. The behaviors that need strengthening are Melissa's willingness to put her dirty clothes in the hamper and to put her toys back in the toy box rather than leaving them scattered everywhere. We know that praise, attention, and a parent's recognition when the child does these things will strengthen them. But it may be the case that Melissa never picks up after herself at present, so the parent would have very little opportunity to start using that praise.

How can we get Melissa to start making the effort? The first step consists of thinking of things the child really enjoys doing that can be used as reinforcers. Melissa's Mom probably knows the kind of things her daughter likes to do, such as watching favorite programs on television, staying up until 8:30 (rather than her usual bedtime of 8:00), or playing a special game in the evening with her parents. Any of these can serve as a reinforcer, provided (1) Melissa enjoys the activity, (2) access to it can be made to depend on whether Melissa first does the task we are asking of her, and (3) the parent is willing to allow her daughter to engage in the special activity if the child first completes her end of the deal by cleaning up after herself.

The second step is to set up a few rules or guidelines to establish a relationship between enjoyable activities (the rewards) and the child's actions we want to see strengthened. If watching television after dinner is an activity that Melissa enjoys, Mom could have a conversation with her daughter that sounds something like this:

"Melissa, all of us in the family have responsibilities or chores we need to do. I go to work some of the day, I keep the house clean, and I fix most of our meals. Those are my jobs. At night, after I've done them, I like to relax, watch television, and read.

"Now you're getting to be a big girl and you're grown up enough to have some of your own responsibilities. It will help me a lot if you make sure your dirty clothes are in the hamper and all your toys are put away right after supper. I know you can do it every day. So I'm going to remind you to do these things just once after dinner, and I want you to do them right away. Then, after you've picked up the clothes in your room and all your toys, you can watch TV. But you won't be able to watch television until everything's picked up. That's our new rule: we all do our jobs first, and then we watch TV."

The parent here is explaining a reward system that will strengthen the child's good behavior patterns. In essence, she is describing a plan in which the youngster can earn an enjoyable activity or privilege through improved conduct. If watching television is something Melissa really enjoys, and if the parent permits the youngster to watch TV only when the chore is completed, a strong positive incentive for good behavior now exists. As you might suspect, the approach of allowing a child to earn some special privilege for good behavior works only for children old enough to understand this kind of "if . . .

then" relationship. Many youngsters older than four can grasp this notion if it is presented in simple terms. For younger children, using immediate praise and attention to reward good behavior is the most effective approach.

Throughout this book we will be applying this general approach to many of the behavior problems children exhibit. If a problem is caused because a child is not now doing something he should be doing, an effective and positive way to solve the problem is by arranging a plan for the youngster to be reinforced for better behavior. Attention and praise from the parent for improved conduct is always a part of that plan, but a parent can motivate his or her child even more effectively by allowing the child to earn special rewards, privileges, or activities through good behavior.

LEARNING HOW TO REWARD YOUR CHILD'S GOOD CONDUCT

Every parent, at one time or another, has probably tried using rewards to motivate a child's good behavior. In our clinic, when this approach to solving children's problems is first explained, I sometimes hear parents say their children "just don't respond" to positive incentives of any kind. While the idea of reinforcing a youngster's good behavior seems remarkably simple and almost foolproof, actually carrying out a plan to solve specific problems requires that the parent understand some important principles for changing children's behavior. Let's review the major principles for successfully using rewards to solve a youngster's behavior problems:

Principle 1: Be very clear about what you are expecting of your youngster.

Principle 2: Reinforcement must be rewarding to your child.

Principle 3: Earning special rewards should depend on your child's good behavior.

Principle 4:   If you use tangible rewards, always couple them with your own praise and recognition of the child's actions.

Principle 5:   Rewards should quickly follow your child's good behavior.

Principle 6:   Focus on only one problem at a time.

Principle 7:   Be consistent.

Learn to think in terms of specific actions you would like to see your child exhibit. When we begin talking with the parents of a child who exhibits behavior problems, the parents often tell us they want their youngster to "act better," "take more responsibility for himself," or "be cooperative." These are all common problems, but they are also phrased in very general ways. A parent might know what "being good" or "taking responsibility" mean, but the child may not understand what is being expected by his parents. Before you can develop a plan to reinforce your child's good behavior, it's important to identify clearly what actions you want to see happen more often.

According to his father, six-year-old Jamie is "impossible and argumentative" every night. When we asked the parent to be more specific, he told us the boy hated getting ready for bed and would stall as long as possible in the evening to avoid those things he needed to do before bedtime. Every night, either Jamie's mother or his father would end up nagging him to brush his teeth, to bathe, and to get in his pajamas. When Jamie ignored his parents (as he often did at such times), arguments would begin between everyone in the family. On a typical night it took almost an hour of parental reminding, then nagging, and then demanding before Jamie would grudgingly get ready for bed.

When these parents first talked with us, they phrased their problems broadly (being "impossible" and "argumentative") and imprecisely. To develop a workable plan for changing a child's behavior problems, we need to identify which actions the parent wants to see, because they are really the cause of the problem. In this case, Jamie's unwillingness to get ready for bed on his own (or, more specifically, his unwillingness to brush his teeth, wash, and get into his pajamas) seemed to be causing most of the difficulties. Those are the actions we would seek to change by developing a plan to reinforce the youngster for getting ready on time and without excessive reminding from his parents. (In this case the problem was quickly solved by letting Jamie earn the privilege of staying up a half hour past his usual bedtime of 8:00 if he brushed his teeth, bathed, and put on pajamas with only one reminder; if he didn't do those things, he had to go to bed a half hour earlier than his usual bedtime.)

Our point here is that you, as a parent, can learn to solve your child's behavior problems most effectively if you are able to identify, in fairly clear and objective behavioral terms, what you want your child to do differently. Once you can specify the actions that need to take place, it is possible to develop a concrete plan that will encourage those actions.

Arrange for your child's good behavior to be followed by rewarding consequences. Even when the parent has clearly identified the desired behavior, there must still be some incentive in order for the child to actually perform well. As we have already pointed out, many parents make the mistake of failing to sufficiently notice and reward their children's desirable conduct when it does take place. The best way for a parent to encourage a child's good behavior isn't by lecturing the youngster, isn't by scolding or nagging, and isn't by threatening the child with a spanking. It is by helping the child learn that his good behavior will be reciprocated by positive reactions, including praise and even special privileges or other rewards.

You know your child best and probably have a good idea of what activity your child would enjoy as a reward for better behavior. Examples of tangible rewards and privileges that are effective for many children include being allowed to stay up a bit later than the usual bedtime; having a story read at bedtime by the parent; having a special time with Mom or Dad to play a game, play catch, or work on a favorite craft; watching television; having a special snack; earning a small allowance (for older children); and having time to play a special game.

Your own child may respond to some of these privileges, or different events may be more potent reinforcers. Try asking the child what special things he would enjoy; kids are often able to tell their parents what special privileges they would most like to be able to earn. Notice how your child likes to spend his time when he can do anything he wants. Does the youngster immediately head for the television set? If so, it's a good bet that TV watching is a reinforcing activity for him or for her. Does he like to play a certain game, read picture or comic books, or like to stay up late? If a child seeks out certain activities or privileges on his own, and if you don't find them objectionable, it is reasonable to consider them as possible rewards. Our aim, then, is to establish a planned and formalized program so the child can start to earn favorite privileges by behaving well.

Special rewards should depend on your child's good behavior. If we make access to special privilege dependent on a child's good behavior, it is important that those special outcomes occur only when the child exhibits improved behavior. Returning once again to the example of Melissa, if watching television in the evening is something she can do regardless of whether her toys are picked up after dinner, no relationship is established between the good behavior and the proposed incentive; she gets to watch television anyway. Or, if Jamie can manage to stay up until 8:30 even if he didn't get ready for bed with only one reminder, that incentive loses its specialness and its meaning.

There are two practical points here for parents to keep in mind. The first is that if you offer your child the opportunity to earn a special reward through good behavior, make certain the incentive is something you are in a position to control, so the child is sure to receive it when his behavior is good but not when his behavior is bad. Second, don't plan to use as special incentives things that you would certainly give your youngster anyway. For a privilege to be special, it needs to be something your youngster will really enjoy when he has earned it.

FIGURE I

Arranging a Plan to Reinforce and
Strengthen Your Child's Good Behavior

First, think of the problem you are having with your child. Is it being caused because the youngster doesn't now do something you feel is reasonable and appropriate to expect? If so, a reinforcement plan to encourage that action will probably help.

Second, decide exactly what it is you want your child to do. Explain to the child what you expect of him in clear and specific terms. Focus on only one problem at a time.

Third, think of some special activity or reward that your child can earn by engaging in the good behavior you've just identified. Make certain your youngster really enjoys that incentive and will behave well to earn it.

Fourth, remember always to communicate your praise and recognition when the child exhibits the desired behavior. Tangible privileges or rewards never take the place of your recognition; they are only extra incentives. For children who are only three or four years old, your praise and attention are the most powerful tools for improving behavior.

Fifth, make certain the reward and your praise closely follow the action you are trying to strengthen. Reinforce good behavior immediately and consistently.

If you use tangible items or privileges as rewards, always be sure to couple them with your own praise and recognition of the child's improved behavior. As we have stressed before, your attention and praise are the most powerful tools for strengthening your child's good behavior patterns. Warmly letting a youngster know when he is behaving well, rather than focusing on times of misbehavior, is a strong and lasting strategy for bringing about change in a youngster's conduct. Why, then, should parents use special privileges as further rewards? One reason is simply that they increase the incentive for a youngster to start doing things that are currently avoided. When a child is not doing tasks that are reasonable to expect and when a parent feels increasingly frustrated and critical toward the child, we want to change that negative pattern as quickly as possible. A more general reason is that we usually want children to learn that, throughout life, good actions can result in special recognition and benefits.

On the other hand, we never want children to be motivated only by tangible and external rewards. We certainly don't want children always to expect that they will get something every time they act in a kind, proper, or good manner. That is why spoken recognition from a parent is so important. Early in this chapter we noted that, over time, people acquire the ability to reinforce themselves for their actions. For example, successful students are able to tell themselves "I studied hard for that test and did a good job" even before they get a grade. Successful business people are able to take pride in their work even if their accomplishments go unnoticed by others. And successful and charitable people can quietly do compassionate things for others with the knowledge that they did something good as their only benefit.

How does this important process develop? We now realize that children come to internalize statements made by adults. If a child is told that a certain action is good and worthwhile, eventually the youngster will start to tell himself the same thing even when the parent is no longer present. When a parent says, "Tom, I'm very proud that you helped your younger brother get dressed this morning; that's what big brothers are for," the child will be in a position to incorporate that same statement in his own mind and, in the future, actually tell himself something similar to guide his own actions (such as, "It's a good thing to help my brother when he needs it").

When a child has behaved well, is praised, and is given a reason why his action was good, it forms the foundation for the child's ability to monitor his own future actions and derive self-gratification for behaving well. If a parent only provides a privilege or external reward for good behavior and forgets to praise the child's actions in words, this exceedingly important benefit is lost. The internalization process does not develop immediately, and children don't tell themselves all the statements they are casually told by others. But when a parent learns to routinely provide verbal praise and explanation along with earned special privileges in direct response to good behavior, this positive reaction exerts a strong influence on the child's conduct.

A final reason why parental praise is important involves the fact that earning special privileges through good behavior will eventually be discontinued. Melissa won't always get to watch television only if she has picked up her room, and Jamie won't always get to stay up an extra half hour by getting ready for bed on time. What parents really want is for their children to listen to them. Once a reinforcement-based program of special privileges and plenty of parent praise is initiated, the child often eventually gains more satisfaction from earning positive recognition from the parent than from the special privilege with which this positive recognition has been paired.

Rewards should quickly follow a child's good behavior.

"If you play with your little sister all week without fighting, I'll take you both to the zoo."

"I know that you can use the bathroom when you need to. So as soon as you show me how grown-up you are by not having an accident for three whole days in a row, we'll go out and look for that two-wheeler bike."

Each of these sounds like the start of an effective and positive reward system in which the child's good behavior will result in some consequence the child enjoys. They are the kind of "if . . . then" statements many parents use when they want their children to behave better. There is, however, a problem in these examples that will seriously reduce their effectiveness: The rewarding outcome is simply too far removed, too distant, from the child's behavior.

Most adults have the ability to delay gratification for a relatively long time. We can study each day for exams in college that are still a month away, we can work on business reports that our bosses may not evaluate for weeks, and we can put a little money into Christmas Club savings accounts each week beginning in January. In short, we can do things well ahead of when we will be able to enjoy the fruits of our efforts. Children, however, are much more oriented toward the present and the very near future. Expecting the actions of a three-year-old, or even a six-year-old, to be strongly influenced by the possibility of some benefit in the distant future is unrealistic. For a young child, the distant future isn't very far away. Any plan to reinforce a child's good behavior works best when the incentive closely follows the action we seek to strengthen. When you praise a child's good conduct, your recognition should be given either while the child is behaving well or immediately after you noticed what the youngster did.

When earning special privileges or rewards is part of a good behavior program, the special privilege should also closely follow the action you want to strengthen. For a young child, any reward should always be given the same day that the privilege was earned. That's why Jamie, when he got ready for bed on his own, earned the right to stay up a little later that same evening. Similarly, Melissa's privilege of watching television occurred right after her clothes and toys were picked up following dinner. The longer the gap between the occurrence of the child's good behavior and the enjoyment of special privilege, the less effective the privilege will be. That's why it is far better to use small daily rewards for good behavior, as opposed to offering a youngster some large reward in the distant future.

Focus on solving just one problem at a time. When we at the clinic first talk with the parents of children with behavior problems, it is not unusual for them to give us a long list of child misbehaviors they would like to see changed. In an extreme case, a parent might tell us that her child won't follow directions and requests, always fights with his brothers, dawdles in the morning when the parent has to take the youngster to daycare, won't go to bed on time, and wets the bed. Understandably, the parent wants to solve all these problems. But just as behavior problems don't usually develop all at once, they cannot all be solved at one time either.

The approach we suggest is learning to focus on solving just one or two specific problems at a time. If there is only one problem that concerns you, that is all you need to work on. But if your youngster has several areas in which his good behavior needs strengthening, pick only one to receive all your attention until it is resolved. In the above example, we might suggest that the parent elect to work only on the child's bedwetting or only on his morning dawdling until the problem is successfully handled. Then attention can be focused on a remaining problem.

As we will see in the chapters on handling specific kinds of behavior problems, most of our approaches do require fairly intensive work on the part of the parent as well as the child. If a parent tries to divide his or her attention across too many different problem areas at once, it will be difficult for the parent to notice and praise the child's improved conduct in each one.

Also, asking a young child to earn some special privilege by doing many different things well each day almost always confuses the child and leads to problems. It is better to work on one single action at a time.

THE IMPORTANCE OF BEING CONSISTENT

As you begin to develop new ways of handling your child's behavior problems, whether you're working on a plan to strengthen better behavior or a new method for discipline (such as we will discuss in chapter 3), it is extremely important to be consistent. One of the very worst things a parent can do is handle a child's misbehavior differently each time it happens. If a parent responds to a child's action on one occasion with praise and a special earned privilege but on a second occasion fails to notice the youngster's behavior, the child won't be able to tell whether what he did was really important. To avoid this, when you develop a plan to change some problematic aspect of your child's conduct, it should be thought of as the way you will handle that problem from now on. Looking back to Jamie, we advised his parents to tell the boy that every night he got ready for bed with only the one reminder he could stay up until 8:30, but that every night he didn't do the required tasks, bedtime would be 7:30. This, in essence, became a "house rule."

We suggest only two exceptions to this consistency principle. First, the exact actions needed to earn a privilege can be changed at some point if it becomes desirable or necessary. For example, if Jamie's bedtime behavior became permanently improved to the point that it could be maintained through parent praise alone but a new problem needed attention, then the child's responsibilities to earn the staying-up-late privilege could also be changed. Second, if Jamie for some reason lost interest in staying up late and it ceased to be a reward in his eyes, a new privilege (mutually agreeable to the parents and child) could be substituted. However, the basic framework of our problem-solving approach — specifically reinforcing the child's desired behavior on a consistent basis — is maintained.

TEN CONCERNS PARENTS MOST OFTEN HAVE ABOUT REWARD-BASED PROGRAMS TO INCREASE THEIR CHILDREN'S GOOD BEHAVIOR

1. Rewarding a child for behaving well, especially with things like special privileges, sounds like bribery. I'd hate to bribe my child into behaving well. The use of special and concrete positive consequences to promote good behavior is a principle by which the world operates. Think of yourself and your own experiences. You probably didn't feel you were being bribed when you were given an A on a paper or exam in school; you felt, instead, that this reward was something you earned through your own efforts. Similarly, most of us don't feel we've been bribed if we receive a merit raise or bonus from our employers at the end of a good work year. It is interesting to note that schools and employers that don't provide this kind of special recognition (the so-called ungraded schools or the companies where everyone gets the same raise regardless of effort) tend to have morale and motivation problems because people feel their actions don't get recognized. Children, in the same way, don't learn to engage in good behavior and don't develop positive feelings of success, competence, and skill unless they receive positive recognition for their actions.

Bribery *is* bad. But bribery occurs when a parent first gives a child something in return for the youngster's promise to behave well later ("Tommy, I'll let you go to the park if you promise never to throw a tantrum again"). The rationale for reinforcement is the opposite of bribery; here, the child earns a special privilege or reward only by first showing that he can behave well. That's an important difference.

2. *It still bothers me to reward my child for behaving well.*
Children, except for those who are raised in an extremely neglectful environment, always get attention, notice, and comment from their parents. This attention, however, often occurs when the child has misbehaved or is in the process of misbehaving. Structured reward programs of the kind we advocate change this pattern by providing special positive attention not when the child misbehaves, but when the child behaves well. Thus, these systems strengthen the child's patterns of desirable behavior, permit the child to develop feelings of competency and self-esteem, and show the child that it is possible to elicit positive responses from the parent.

3. *I've tried before to reward my child's good behavior, but it just doesn't seem to work for him.* Almost all parents have at some time attempted reward-based programs to increase a child's appropriate behavior; many of these attempts *are* unsuccessful. The reasons for past lack of success vary, but often include the failure to specify exactly what behaviors the child is expected to exhibit, attempting to change too many behaviors at once, failure to reinforce the child in a way that is sufficiently rewarding in his eyes, inconsistency, and abandoning the system before it has had a chance to be effective. Usually when parents tell us they have already tried rewarding their child's good behavior, they have done so only in a casual, informal manner, rather than with the more structured and consistent kind of plan we advocate.

4. *I know this sounds terrible to say, but at times it seems like my child does almost nothing well and always misbehaves. I'm going to have trouble finding any good behavior to reinforce.*
When a child's behavior problems are longstanding and wide-ranging, a parent can begin to feel not only pessimistic but also somewhat angry toward the child. This is all the more reason to begin using a reward-based program — it will prove to both you and your child that things can be different and your interactions can be more positive. Remember that the focus of

a good behavior program is the kind of conduct the child now demonstrates too infrequently. The most important requirement is that the actions you specify as desirable be things the child *can* do. For example, you would not require a young child to put on a buttoned shirt by himself as part of a "get-yourself-dressed" plan until you are certain he can manage this.

5. *Is it reasonable to arrange a plan where my child gets to earn a special privilege (and my praise) simply for being good all day?* This is a strategy that some parents try on their own, with a reward of some kind being offered to the child for "behaving well," "acting grown-up," or even "not bothering Mom." The problem with this strategy is vagueness, because it is not being made clear exactly what the child must do in order to "behave well" or "act grown-up." Reinforcement approaches are most effective when a child has a specific responsibility that must be completed to earn the special reward.

6. *Programs to reward children's good behavior seem somewhat structured and controlling. How do children respond emotionally to this approach?* Approaches of the kind we advocate are structured and do directly change the child's behavior. That is why they work and why they are more effective than indirect and inconsistent approaches. They also help a child to learn, under conditions of positive reinforcement rather than excessive punishment or criticism — that he can become responsible for his own actions. Because the approach is based on positive recognition for good behavior, children generally respond to it favorably and often consider it a good behavior "game." While there has not been a great deal of research in this area, many psychologists believe that children whose parents used reward-based systems grow up more secure, more confident, more responsible, and more creative than children whose parents do not use these approaches.

7. *It seems as though the parent has a great deal of the responsibility for carrying out this kind of program, when it is*

the child who has the behavior problem. Is this impression correct? The parent does have the major responsibility for planning the good behavior program and for arranging positive consequences as the child's behavior improves. As we discussed earlier, this is because parents are in the position to arrange for positive consequences that foster the child's development of desirable behavior, the learning of new skills, and the decrease of excessive misbehaviors. While the behavior problem may be the child's, it is the parent who is in a position to help solve those problems. It does take the parent a certain amount of time, effort, and attention and requires a willingness to change the way misbehaviors are handled. But compared to the amount of time and energy that parents can spend worrying about their child's actions or repeatedly trying things that don't work, these new strategies often succeed quickly.

8. When I have arranged for a good behavior plan — identified desirable behaviors, selected reinforcers, and read about how to handle specific behavior problems such as those discussed later in the book — how do I explain the system to my child? First, it is desirable to include the child in your planning even before you arrange the final program that will go into effect. We often advise the parent to sit down with the child and explain that you want the child's assistance in developing a plan to help things go smoother at home and that you think the child should be able to earn some extra privileges for his help. This is a good time to explore potential reinforcers to which your child will respond (such as a daily allowance to be spent any way the child wants, staying-up-late privileges, special treats, and so on). If possible, let the child help you to decide what reinforcers will be made available. Next, explain your thoughts about those responsibilities or behaviors that will earn the day's rewards. Keep in mind that a program should be clear, uncomplicated, and workable. (We will be reviewing specific approaches that work best for various behavior problems in later chapters.)

Always present good behavior programs to the child in a positive way. Remember, this will be a way for the child to earn extra privileges or treats, and it should never be presented as a you-do-this-or-else proposition. The child should be told, ahead of time, about how the program will work, what privileges will follow completion of the good behavior, and that those benefits will not occur unless the child meets that day's goal.

9. Do good behavior programs bring about change immediately? In many cases almost immediate improvement occurs. Occasionally, however, there will be a period when the child initially acts worse. This most often occurs when the new approach is first started. Whenever a parent changes the way he or she acts toward a child, the child may test the new approach to see how the parent will respond. Parents who don't expect this may be taken by surprise and, even worse, may too quickly change what might have been an effective system. If this temporary worsening occurs, keep following whatever consequences you have established. If the child fails to earn the day's allowance, he should not get it that day. If TV watching or staying up later were agreed upon as good behavior consequences, they should not be allowed. Do not get angry with the child or change the system; simply remind the child that he or she will have an opportunity to earn the rewards the next day. When they do finally occur, praise the child strongly, clearly conveying your pleasure at the child's improved behavior, and provide the reward as promised.

If a good behavior plan has been in effect for a reasonable length of time (let's say one week) and there is still no change, the parent should review its fundamentals. The most likely stumbling blocks are these: (1) The rewards that follow the child's good behavior are too weak or simply unimportant to the child. You may need to develop stronger and more desirable rewards that will provide a greater incentive; (2) The child can enjoy the special privilege reinforcers whether or not he behaves well. Here you will need to tighten the system so that the special rewards are available only when the child's behavior warrants them; (3) The system may be overly complex rather than focusing on only one problem at a time.

10. Once I begin a program to systematically reinforce my child's appropriate behavior, how long will it need to be continued? As we have already noted, the rationale for a reward-based program is to strengthen good behavior in a highly consistent and powerful manner. The formal program itself should be continued as long as necessary for the new and more positive behavior patterns to become well-established and routine for the child. If the program is discontinued too soon (such as immediately after improvement in the behavior problems takes place), the initial problems may well recur. Don't be in too great a hurry to change any system that is working. We often suggest that parents continue a good reinforcement program for at least one month *after* the program has become successful.

On the other hand, a parent will want to eventually phase out the tangible incentives used in a behavior program. We recommend a two-step process for doing this. First, the parent should continue to praise the child's appropriate and desired behavior throughout the time that a program is in effect; this is a cardinal rule for the reasons we discussed earlier. As tangible rewards are gradually reduced, continued positive comment and praise from the parent will serve to maintain the child's actions. At the same time parental attention is maintained, the special-privilege incentives can gradually be reduced. One way to do this is by using tangible rewards only at the end of a successful week, rather than at the end of each successful day. You might, for example, want to negotiate some special activity that the child values when a week of good behavior has occurred.

This leads us to a final point. Once improvement in child behavior has taken place, and once these patterns have become well-established, it is still important to continue your positive verbal recognition of the child's good behavior. When new actions are first being learned by the child, it is desirable to reinforce them every time they occur. This strengthens new behavior most quickly. Later, but only once these actions have become established, you needn't praise your child every time they occur, but rather on an occasional basis. When your child has reached the point where your periodic praise maintains his continued good actions, the child's behavior problem has probably been solved.

3/

Discipline That Instructs Rather Than Punishes

AS we saw in the last chapter, behavior problems can come about because a child isn't doing certain things a parent has the right to expect. In these cases, developing an approach that reinforces the child's desirable conduct is the key to solving the problem. But as all parents know, there are times when behavior problems consist of what the child does rather than what he doesn't do. Here the task isn't only strengthening a child's good behavior pattern but also altering a misbehavior pattern. By far the most common misbehaviors parents want to see changed are their children's fighting, tantrumming, destructiveness, and noncompliance with what parents feel are reasonable requests. And by far the two most common means that parents use to handle these kinds of problems are scolding and spanking.

Scolding, as we use the term here, means telling a child that you are displeased with something he just did. Usually parents scold their children's misbehavior when they are frustrated and angry but not angry enough to spank. Instead, they might tell the child something like, "Tom, don't ever get mad and throw your toys around like that," or "Stop having temper tantrums when we go to the store — it really makes me unhappy," or "You'll get a spanking if you ever do that again." As we will discuss shortly, it is occasionally useful and necessary to give children feedback about their behavior (although it's best to combine negative comments like those above with some advice about how you want the child to behave differently in the future). But parents who find they must continually ask, tell, nag, or even yell at their children not to do certain things are over-using scolding as a disciplinary technique.

If you are a scolder, you probably already know that it doesn't work very well. As we saw in the last chapter, scolding provides attention for misbehaving youngsters, and because it is the misbehavior that gains this attention, scolding can actually reinforce the child's misconduct. To make matters worse, parents who routinely scold their children become accustomed to focusing on the negative, noticing when the youngster misbehaves but failing to see and strengthen the child's good behavior. Kids learn simply to ignore scoldings. If a parent rarely scolds a child, the youngster is apt to pay attention when the parent must tell the child he did something wrong. But if a youngster always hears nags, reminders, criticisms, and other don'ts, he gets so used to hearing them that they are eventually ignored.

Finally, scolding can harm both parent and youngster. Parents who find themselves frequently scolding their children begin to feel like bad parents because their nagging isn't really changing their child's conduct. And because children have a way of living up to (or down to) their parents' expectations, kids who are routinely reminded they are acting badly tend to keep doing just that.

When scolding doesn't work, the common next step that parents take when their child continues to misbehave is spanking.

SPANKING: WHEN IT WORKS AND WHEN IT DOESN'T WORK

One of the questions most frequently asked of child psychologists is whether children should be spanked. The answer is yes, but not nearly as often as parents ordinarily think necessary. The reason why parents should not spank excessively goes beyond the value judgment that it is undesirable for parents to control children by physical force, in essence a kind of violence. Routine spanking for misbehavior is simply a much less effective child management strategy than some other techniques we will be describing shortly. But before we talk about alternatives to spanking, let's look at those occasions when spanking is appropriate.

In our clinic, we suggest that children should be spanked when they are doing something that could cause injury to the child or to someone else. Spanking is indicated when a child starts running toward a busy street, is reaching up to pull a hot pan off the stove, is about to stick a fork into an electric outlet (or chew on an appliance cord), or is trying to topple an infant's high chair (with the infant in it). These are the kinds of misbehaviors that need to be stopped immediately and in such a way that they will not recur, because the child's safety is at stake. Spanking is the best technique to use in this kind of situation.

When a child must be spanked for these reasons, parents should follow some general principles:

A spank should immediately follow the child's dangerous behavior. The ideal time to spank is just when the child is starting to engage in the dangerous act or immediately after you observe it. If your child is young and if the punishment is delayed by more than a few moments, it will probably be ineffective. The immediacy and suddenness of a spank are what make it work.

A spank should consist of one or two swats with an open hand, preferably on the child's bottom. If a spank is to be effective, it must be intense enough to cause the child brief discomfort. If it is too light, the spank will not actually be a punishment. Never, however, should spanking consist of an extended series of hits, never should it include shaking the child, and never should it involve using any object with which to spank the child. One or two open-handed swats on the bottom are all that is needed when a child is about to do something dangerous. Spanking rituals (such as whipping with a belt against a child's bare bottom) are unnecessary and may be emotionally harmful to the child.

Spank first, explain why immediately after. When a child is doing something that is dangerous and must be stopped immediately, you should also deliver the spank immediately. Tell the child no as you swat his bottom, but save your explanation until afterward. Some parents explain, in elaborate terms, why the child is to be spanked before the spanking. This is risky because it separates the spank from the dangerous action we want to eliminate, and the immediacy of the punishment is very important. After one or two swats on the bottom, give your child a rationale for the punishment, one that is simple enough to be easily understood. Along with it, be sure to tell the child what new action is more acceptable (such as, "Don't ever run into the street — it's dangerous and can hurt you. I'd really like to see you play in the yard instead"). Then forget the incident and encourage your child to play in an acceptable, safe fashion.

Many parents, including some of the best-intentioned people in the world, overuse spanking to control their children's everyday misbehaviors. When a parent finds it necessary to spank a child for such things as tantrums, noncompliance, aggressiveness, talking back, not carrying out expected responsibilities, and similar things, too much spanking is going on and a number of problems can develop:

1. Children get used to frequent physical punishment (such as spanking) so that it is no longer effective. The first few times a child is spanked, it works. But after spanking becomes more commonplace, the child will adapt to the punishment and it becomes increasingly less effective. The parent then has to spank more (or harder) to get progressively less effect. That is why spanking is best left for the few and critical situations described earlier.

2. Spanking only teaches a child what not to do; it does not help the child learn better behavior. Even if spanking *were* effective as a routine form of discipline, another major problem remains. Punishment of this kind can eliminate bad behavior but cannot teach the child good habits to substitute for the bad actions. This is one of the reasons that children whose parents rely on spanking as a disciplinary technique have to be spanked quite often. If a child learns only to stop behaving badly but not what is a more acceptable way of acting, long-term improvement is unlikely. Because other forms of discipline can combine reduction of bad behavior with increases in good behavior, they are much more effective than spanking.

3. Spanking and other physical forms of punishment increase the child's own level of aggressiveness. Children whose misbehavior is controlled through physical punishment tend to be more aggressive children, and tend to grow to be more aggressive adolescents and adults, than children not disciplined through physical force. This finding, which is supported by several studies, tends to disprove the widely held belief that stern discipline can somehow build a child's character. It is not uncommon for parents who frequently spank their children to one day find them swinging right back.

4. Spanking's effects tend to be temporary. When a child is spanked often for a certain misbehavior, he or she may learn to suppress that misbehavior when the parent is present. This does not mean that the child will actually stop misbehaving; he will just be more careful to notice whether the parent is watching before he does it.

5. Because parents don't like to spank their children, they may fail to discipline misbehavior consistently. No good parent wants to spank his or her child. Spanking is unpleasant for both child and parent. As a result, parents may wait until the child's behavior gets bad enough to merit spanking before they intervene at all. Under these circumstances, the parent is not using more moderate forms of effective discipline before the child's behavior gets out of control but instead is waiting until a crisis develops and then stopping it with a spanking. What is needed is a set of techniques that can be used to control the child's misbehavior before it reaches the point where spanking seems to be the parent's only choice.

THREE WAYS TO REDUCE CHILDREN'S MISBEHAVIORS WITHOUT SPANKING

Three practical ways for parents to reduce their children's acting-out misbehaviors without resorting to physical punishment are (1) ignoring minor misbehavior, (2) using a technique called time-out, and (3) reducing misbehavior by rewarding good behavior. These techniques offer a number of advantages over spanking. While they teach a child right from wrong, they go beyond reducing bad behavior and also strengthen good behavior in its place. In general, they lead to more durable and long-lasting improvement in the child's behavior than spanking does. And because the techniques themselves aren't harsh and unpleasant, parents are more likely to use them consistently. Let's review how each of these techniques works. In later chapters we'll apply them to specific kinds of behavior problems.

STRATEGY 1: IGNORING MINOR MISBEHAVIOR

In chapter 2 we discussed in some detail how a parent can foster a child's good behavior by seeing that rewards (including parental recognition and attention) immediately follow the desired action. Because a parent's attention serves as a reward or reinforcer to most children, actions that get the parent's attention will tend to be repeated in the future. We can take that same principle and turn it around to reduce the incidence of child misbehaviors. If parental attention and recognition can maintain a child's good actions, *removing* that attention when the child misbehaves can decrease the frequency of problem behaviors.

Let's look at two of our clinic cases to illustrate how parental attention maintains some behavior problems:

A young couple reported having a problem with their son, Johnny, now just over three years old. The difficulty was the child's crying at night. Johnny did not like to go to bed, and after a few minutes in bed would begin to cry. The parents first thought something might be physically wrong with the child and took him to the doctor to make certain he wasn't ill. The pediatrician pronounced Johnny in perfect health and referred the family to us. We focused attention in our interview on finding out how the parents handled Johnny's nighttime crying. They reported various approaches. On some occasions they tried to ignore the crying as long as possible. At other times they let Johnny get out of bed and watch television with them for a few minutes. This would temporarily stop his crying, although it generally resumed shortly after he went back to the bedroom. When the parents became particularly frustrated by the late-night upsets, they scolded him severely. Unfortunately, this only made him cry more.

A second family's problem illustrates a similar kind of difficulty:

Mr. and Mrs. Baker were most concerned about their six-year-old boy's moral behavior. The parents were extremely conservative individuals who placed a high value on propriety, their religious faith, and concern about others. Recently, their son Timothy had begun to say things that startled and upset them. Several days earlier, for example, the parents had asked Timothy to stop watching television and get ready for bed. The child answered that he wanted to stay up late and watch the whole movie. When the parents explained that he could not do that on a school night, Timothy became angry and yelled "I hate you! And I hate God, too!" The child had done this a number of times, usually when he was mad at his parents. On other occasions he used profanities the parents found objectionable. Mr. Baker mentioned that Timothy often watched his parents intently immediately after these outbursts, apparently to gauge their reaction to what he said.

In both examples, the misbehavior was actually being perpetuated by the ways the parents handled it. Johnny, who cried at night, seemed to be doing so because he was being reinforced for it: the parents, more often than not, *did* come to his room when he was tantrumming and provided recognition of his misbehavior. Sometimes they actually let him get up and watch TV. While parents should always check on the nighttime crying of infants or very young children (since crying is one of the only ways infants can communicate), Johnny had learned to cry and tantrum in order to manipulate his parents. Johnny found that by crying long enough, he might eventually get to leave the bedroom. The parents, in their attempt to stop the child's bedtime crying, were actually maintaining it by rewarding the misbehavior!

In Timothy's case it was evident to us that the child had zeroed in, with remarkable skill, on a sensitive area that was certain to provoke a reaction from his parents. In order to get back at them when he was angry, he learned to say things his parents found upsetting, things that would draw a startled but attentive response.

In both cases our advice to the parents was straightforward: they should withhold attention and recognition from the child whenever he was misbehaving. We advised Johnny's parents to ignore his nighttime crying, provided they were certain the boy was not ill, fearful, or otherwise carrying on for a real reason. And we told Timothy's parents to totally ignore him when he made comments intended to upset them. By withholding social recognition for the misconduct; this misconduct, rendered pointless, would then disappear.

When we instructed Timothy's parents to ignore his comments about hating them, they were at first reluctant to do this.

They felt that *not* reacting would convey to the child that they approved of his action. They also felt that their current reaction to the child's defiant talk (scolding, telling the youngster that they were upset and disappointed in him, or threatening spanking) should be punishing to the boy. Our analysis of the situation told us just the opposite. While the parents felt that their negative reaction to the child's misbehavior was punishing, Timothy was really trying to get just that reaction from them. If he were to find out that they wouldn't react to him at all when he talked this way, the purpose of his misbehavior would be gone and he would have no reason to continue it.

Since Johnny was crying at night in an effort to get his parents' attention (and, he hoped, to be able to leave the bedroom), our advice that the parents ignore the crying was designed to prevent this misbehavior from being rewarded. When Johnny learned that bedtime meant bedtime, and that crying would neither change it nor gain special attention from his parents, the crying would stop and would in time cease being a behavior problem.

In order to ignore child misbehaviors and make them go away, parents should understand that:

This approach works best for behavior problems that come about when the child is either trying to irritate the parent or when he wants something unreasonable and feels he can get it by bugging his father or mother. The aim here is to break the connection between the child's misbehavior and the parental attention that the child is really trying to gain through that misbehavior. Crying when the child wants something unreasonable, minor forms of talking back, or repeatedly asking the same question to bother the parent ("Why can't I stay up late? Why? Why? Why can't I?") are all common problems that can be made worse if the parent keeps attending to them. We suggest that the parent explain to the child once what the parent's position will be ("Johnny, it's your bedtime now. If you stay up late you won't be able to get up in the morning. So if you want to cry tonight in bed, you'll still have to stay there."). Then ignore the continued crying or other misbehavior.

Ignore only the specific misbehavior you want to see reduced; never ignore your child generally. Your aim is to remove attention, notice, and recognition of certain specific misbehaviors, not to ignore your child by giving him or her the silent treatment for extended periods of time. If you are ignoring some form of backtalk or other spoken misbehavior, act as though you don't hear the child for several minutes following the misbehavior and give the child no attention during this interval. If you are ignoring your child's crying, pay no attention and give no recognition to the child while he is crying and for a couple of minutes afterward. Again, you aren't trying to punish the child by ignoring him for long periods — what you are doing is making certain no attention of any kind will accompany the specific misbehavior you want to reduce.

Just as you are removing attention for specific misbehaviors, supply plenty of extra attention when the child is behaving well. In Timothy's case we told the parents to ignore his I-hate-you comments and to avoid interacting with the child in any way—by not looking at him, talking to him, or reacting emotionally — for a short time after his unacceptable comment. At the same time, the parents were instructed to talk with him, praise his calmed-down behavior, and interact with him warmly once he began acting appropriately again. We suggested that they later tell Timothy that it is fine for him to disagree with them, but only in a normal tone of voice and not by saying "I hate you." When Timothy did express his wants, opinions, or disagreements more acceptably, his parents were told to specifically praise this conduct.

Just as one withholds attention for misbehavior, it is crucial to supply extra attention when the child begins behaving well. This extremely important step tells the child he will still get your recognition and attention. Always find some way to interact positively with your child or find some behavior the child is exhibiting that you can praise within an hour or less of the time that you ignore a misbehavior. In the case of a child like Johnny who cried at night, the parent should ignore the nighttime crying but praise the child the next morning for eventually going to sleep or for going to sleep with less crying than on past nights.

Be prepared for a brief worsening of the child's conduct when you start to ignore a certain misbehavior. Let's return for a moment to the example of Johnny's crying. We told the parents to ignore the child's tantrumming in bed and, in essence, to let him cry himself out and fall asleep without any attention from them. Johnny had already learned, however, that he could get his parents' attention (and perhaps get to stay up late) by crying. So when the parents first started to ignore him, Johnny's most likely thought was "They just haven't heard me yet — I'd better cry louder and longer until they give in."

If Johnny keeps crying, his parents have two choices: either give in or keep ignoring him. They should do the latter. Giving in and providing attention after the child has already been tantrumming in bed for a long while will make it even more difficult to control this behavior problem in the future. The child simply will have learned that he must be loud and persistent to gain attention, and he will cry even longer on later occasions. By continuing to ignore the nighttime crying, even if it means ignoring crying that goes on for thirty minutes, an hour, two hours or more on the first nights, the parent can look forward to a gradual decrease (and then the elimination) of this problem as the child becomes aware that mother or father will not respond to the tantrums. To recap, then, when you decide to systematically ignore a certain misbehavior, (1) expect the possibility of an initial worsening as the child tests you, (2) don't give in and provide attention to the misbehavior, (3) do reinforce and provide special and extra attention for the child's good behavior, and (4) be consistent both in ignoring the misbehavior and in providing extra attention to the child's good behavior.

STRATEGY 2: TIME-OUT — THE ALTERNATIVE TO SPANKING

Ignoring works best for acting-out behavior problems that are intended to get the parent's attention. But in some cases, children misbehave in ways that are too extreme to be ignored. It is at these times, when the parent feels the child needs to be spanked, that an alternative to spanking called *time-out* can be especially effective.

Time-out is a brief period of isolation following a serious misbehavior that would otherwise lead to a spanking. In a way it is a more structured and more effective version of sending a child to his room. The rationale for time-out is simple: Being alone and removed from all sources of attention for even a short time is unpleasant to children. If a certain kind of serious misbehavior is consistently followed by time-out discipline, it will decrease. Moreover, time-out works as well as (or better than) physical punishments like spanking and does so without the unfortunate side-effects of physical discipline.

Because time-out is a powerful technique, we will review it carefully. It is critical for a parent using time-out to follow these guidelines closely:

1. For what misbehaviors should time-out be used? Time-out should be viewed as an alternative to spanking and should be used only for acting-out misbehaviors serious enough to otherwise merit that form of discipline. In our clinic we suggest time-out for children's acts of physical aggression (such as fighting with another child or the parent), destructiveness (such as breaking or aggressively throwing objects), or tantrums that cannot be ignored. Angry bursts of verbal noncompliance with a parent's reasonable request can be dealt with using the time-out, although we suggest that the parent first use a reward-based program to motivate the child's good behavior (as we will discuss in the next section of this chapter). The purpose of time-out is to reduce serious misbehaviors without spanking, not to increase a child's good behavior (by, say, threatening a child with time-out if he doesn't do his homework). Remember, the best way to motivate a child's good behavior is by rewarding, not by threatening. Reserve time-out only for occasions of serious aggression, fighting, destructiveness, or tantrums.

2. For what age children should time-out be used? Time-out, as described here, should be used for children three years and older.

3. Where does time-out take place? The first step for using this procedure consists of finding a spot at home where the child will have to go for his or her time-out. The major requirement of a time-out spot is that it be very dull (with no enjoyable diversions), that it isolate the child from family activities and attention, and that it be safe. Some possibilities might include a hallway, especially if it is out of the way of other family activities or can be closed off with a door; a bathroom that is first made safe by removing all dangerous objects, supplies, or medicines; or a spare bedroom. If these are not practical, an out-of-the-way corner of a little-used room is an acceptable time-out location. Never use any dark, extremely confined, or otherwise scary location for time-out. Places such as closets or small utility rooms that might traumatize a child and cause emotional damage are never permissible. There should be no toys, games, books, television or other fun things in the time-out area. Remember, the only requirements are that the location be isolated from family activities, be dull, and that it be safe.

4. How is time-out used? When the child is misbehaving in one of the ways mentioned, the child should be told once that if the misbehavior continues he or she will go to time-out. If the misbehavior continues after your request for the child to stop, time-out automatically follows. It is best to use time-out quickly, after you've warned the child, rather than waiting until a full-blown tantrum, fight, or destructive episode has already taken place.

The youngster is firmly but unemotionally told he must go to the time-out location you've decided upon. There should be absolutely no discussion with the child about his misbehavior, even if he begins acting better once you've told him to go. Just as spanking, to be effective, must immediately follow a dangerous misbehavior, time-out is an immediate consequence. Time-out does not last very long. In fact, we find it is the consistency and certainty of this penalty, not the length of time the child spends there, that makes it effective. *Children between three and five years of age go to time-out for five minutes; children over five spend one minute in time-out for each year of their age.* Thus, a six-year-old's time-out period is six minutes.

Before using the time-out procedure, buy a small kitchen timer that can be set for the length of time your child will need to spend in time-out. Keep the timer handy near the time-out location. As your child goes into time-out, set the timer for the exact number of minutes he or she will spend there. Tell the child that when the bell rings (but not before), he or she can come out. If time-out is in a room or hallway with a door, shut the door and leave the timer right outside the door so the child can hear it ring. We instruct parents to use the timer for two reasons. First, the child will know that when the bell rings, his period of isolation is over. Second, the parent (who may be angry with the child) will not be tempted to extend time-out for a period longer than it should be. Except under the circumstances we will describe next, the child should *never* be forced to stay in time-out longer than the number of minutes we've just outlined, even if you are very angry.

5. What if my child refuses to go to time-out when I tell him to? This is the most common difficulty parents encounter when first using time-out. It comes about when the child is trying to test you. Once you have told the child he must go to time-out, don't debate with him or allow him to talk you out of it. If the child doesn't go, repeat your request once more. Then tell him calmly but firmly that he will have to spend five extra minutes in time-out for not going when you told him to. If the child still doesn't go, instruct him that it will now be ten additional minutes beyond the original time he must spend there. At this point, if the child still hasn't followed your direction, physically take him to time-out and set the timer for the original period (five minutes or the child's age in minutes) plus the additional ten minutes.

Don't ever allow yourself to chase the child around the room to get him or her into time-out. This focuses attention on the child's misbehavior and can create a game as the youngster tries to evade and agitate you. Time-out should always be handled seriously, calmly, and consistently.

6. What should I do when my child is in time-out? If your child is in time-out and behaving quietly, do nothing at all. This is his or her short period of isolation and you should not interact with the child in any way. Sometimes children will tantrum while they are in time-out to let you know they are angry. Ignore this unless the tantrumming is severe or continues for more than a few minutes. For severe disturbances, go to the door of the time-out location and matter-of-factly tell the child that unless he calms down immediately you will reset the timer to the original period and it will start all over again. Go ahead and do this if the child doesn't become quiet following your warning. If the child leaves the time-out location before his time is up, ask him once to go back. If he does not, take the child back to time-out and reset the timer.

Time-out should be the established period that begins when the child is relatively quiet. If your child talks to you from inside the time-out place while he is there, pay no attention unless he becomes unruly and loud. Then tell him only that you will need to reset the timer unless he becomes quiet. Don't engage in conversation with your child while he's in time-out. Finally, if your child messes up the time-out place while he or she is there, the area must be cleaned up before the youngster comes out.

7. What should I do when the time-out period is over?
When the timer rings, the child can leave time-out. Sometimes children want to show you it didn't bother them and they will stay there after the bell rings. If that happens, just tell your child that he can come out when ready and don't talk to him until he leaves the area.

Once time-out is over, the discipline is over. Calmly tell your child why he or she went to time-out and be sure to explain what you would like the child to do differently in the future. For example, if a child was sent to time-out for hitting her brother, you might say "Gina, you went to time-out for hitting your brother. Please play with him without fighting. If he's doing something that bothers you, tell me rather than hit him." Never continue to scold or punish the child for an incident that has already been disciplined with time-out. Many parents find that the few minutes their child is in time-out gives them the opportunity to calm themselves down following their child's misbehavior.

8. Is there anything else a parent needs to do when using time-out? Yes. As a discipline that reduces a child's misbehaviors, time-out is effective and can almost entirely eliminate the need to spank a child. But it does not, on its own, teach the child to replace the bad actions with better ones, and thus it is only half the total approach a parent needs to use for improving behavior problems. The other half is systematically strengthening the child's good behavior. Whenever time-out is used, the parent should also develop a firm plan for rewarding and increasing good behavior.

We often tell parents that whenever they find it necessary to use a time-out, they should then closely watch their child's activities for the next several hours and notice when the child is behaving well (by playing cooperatively, complying with some request made by the parent, doing a chore, or any other good behavior, even if it is not all that dramatic or unusual). Go out of your way to praise such appropriate and desirable actions as the child exhibits them, and do this more frequently than you normally would. We suggest praising the child at least several times for good behavior during the hours after time-out has been used. This helps your child to learn not only that seriously bad behavior will lead to time-out, but even more important, that good behavior will lead to praise and positive recognition.

9. Does time-out always work? In our clinic, this time-out technique is effective for almost all children who tantrum, are physically aggressive, or are destructive — when it is used consistently and exactly as we've presented it. The parent may at some times encounter difficulties with this technique, however.

FIGURE 2

A Quick Review of Time-Out

1. Reserve time-out only for serious acting-out misbehaviors such as tantrums, fighting, aggressiveness, or intentional destruction of things.
2. Make your time-out location a place that is dull, removed from the center of family activities, but safe and nonfrightening.
3. Make sure time-out immediately follows the serious misbehavior.
4. The time-out period is one minute per year of your child's age, with the exceptions we've noted.
5. Don't talk with your child while he is in time-out.
6. When time-out is over, the punishment is over. Calmly explain to the child why he or she went to time-out and what kind of behavior is acceptable in the future.
7. Make an extra, concerted effort to reward your child's good behavior after using time-out.
8. Be consistent in using time-out and be equally consistent in reinforcing your child's appropriate, positive actions.

If you find it necessary to use time-out more than three times a day, you should consult with a professional about special techniques that may be needed. If your child tantrums so excessively while in time-out that the total period spent there exceeds thirty minutes, or if the child engages in behavior injurious to himself while in isolation, consultation with a professional should be arranged. Chapter 10 discusses how to find this kind of assistance.

STRATEGY 3: LEARN TO REDUCE MISBEHAVIOR BY REWARDING ITS OPPOSITE GOOD BEHAVIOR

A final way to reduce misbehavior can be quite effective, even though it is often overlooked by parents. In fact, the very simplicity of this approach — and the fact that it involves no real punishment — makes it an ideal strategy. This approach requires that we think of a desirable behavior that cannot come about while the child is misbehaving and then set up a plan in which this desirable "opposite" behavior is strongly rewarded. Because a child can't act badly and well at the same time, rewarding the desired conduct will reduce or prevent the undesirable problem behavior. Let's look at an example to see how this can work.

Mrs. Jacobs came to our clinic concerned about a problem she was having with her six-year-old boy and five-year-old girl. As Mrs. Jacobs put it, the two youngsters "can't go for five minutes without fighting with each other." If one child watches TV, the other gets in the way or changes the channel. When she leaves them alone to play, one of the children always runs to her saying he or she has just been hit by the other. Instead of playing co-operatively, the children try to beat one another at the game and both always end up crying. This, according to Mrs. Jacobs, happens all day long.

The situation reported by Mrs. Jacobs is by no means unusual. Many parents become concerned when their children always seem to be fighting with one another. This fighting, then, is the misbehavior we want to reduce. Let's think of its opposite. Clearly, the opposite of fighting is playing together cooperatively and constructively. One way to reduce the children's fighting is to set up a system that strongly rewards and encourages their getting along together.

After school each afternoon, Mrs. Jacobs arranged a "special time" game for her two children. The time was a twenty-minute period when the children would work together on a favorite game or play activity under her watchful eye. During the special time, the children were told that they must play without yelling at one another, hitting, making one another cry, or name-calling. They were to share and play nicely for the whole time. Mom would be listening to see how they did. If the children played appropriately for the twenty minutes and did not fight, both would be reinforced for their good behavior with a special reward or privilege coupled with strong praise. The reward the children could earn here was a special game time with Mom herself, because both youngsters enjoyed this. If either of them fought, called a name, hit, or made the other cry, neither would get the special reward and recognition. We were careful to select a short play period, so that the mother could observe them, and the children were told clearly beforehand which actions were considered acceptable and which unacceptable.

The principles of this approach are those we outlined in chapter 2, with one exception. Here the parent specifically chose to reinforce or reward actions that were incompatible with the children's current habits (fighting). It was now up to the children: they could play appropriately and together earn the special recognition, or they could fight as usual and lose it. To Mrs. Jacobs' surprise (but not to ours), her children elected to play cooperatively during this special time each day, and she never had to resort to threats, spankings, or scoldings. After several successful weeks, the twenty-minute play-together-peacefully period was gradually increased to cover longer periods after school. Once the plan was in effect, Mrs. Jacobs' children gradually learned the important lesson that playing together cooperatively is more fun than the bickering and fighting they had resorted to in the past.

The strategy of reinforcing children for doing something desirable that is the opposite of their current misbehavior works for many problems other than fighting. Some parents, for example, dread taking a young child to a restaurant because they know the youngster will almost immediately get bored sitting at a table and start running around. This problem is hardly unusual; a child under six will normally become bored and a little antsy while sitting at a table for any length of time. Rather than trying to punish a child by scolding or threatening with a spank, it's much easier (and much fairer to the child) for you to take along to the restaurant a small game, puzzle, or book that the youngster enjoys so he will have something to do if he gets bored. You are thus in a position to reinforce your child for doing something acceptable (playing with the puzzle or looking at the book) that is the incompatible opposite of the current behavior problem (in this case, running around a restaurant).

Using this strategy to solve a behavior problem isn't difficult, but it does require some planning ahead on the parent's part. The main steps to follow are these:

1. Think of what your child is now doing that you would like to see happen less often. In the example of Mrs. Jacobs it was her children's fighting and arguing; in the restaurant example it was the youngster's running around. You can probably think of something you would like your own child to do less often, too.

2. Next, and this is the step that requires some ingenuity, decide on an activity you would rather see your youngster do. It should be incompatible with his current misbehavior so that the child can't be doing it and misbehaving

at the same time. Playing cooperatively is the opposite of fighting or arguing, while working a puzzle or looking at a book is the opposite of running around a restaurant. Try to pick an activity that your child likes as a replacement for the present misbehavior.

3. It's always best to provide the youngster with something specific and definite he can do in place of the misbehavior you want to reduce. In the restaurant example, the youngster was given an activity that would occupy his time and attention; he wasn't merely told not to run around. It's much better to redirect a child's activities from a misbehavior to an acceptable behavior than it is to simply tell a child not to misbehave.

4. Once you have explained to your youngster what you would prefer to see him do and actually started him in on the acceptable activity, remember to use the earlier principles we reviewed for strengthening that good behavior. Provide plenty of praise, attention, and approval for your child's more acceptable conduct; let the youngster know you are pleased to see his new actions rather than the old misbehavior; and allow the child to earn some special privilege or reward through behaving well.

As we have seen, the principles of learning from experience can be used to solve many childhood behavior problems. Yet children learn not only from their own personal experiences but also by watching the experiences of others. Let's now see how children learn by observation and how this principle can also be used to solve behavior problems.

4/
Modeling: How Children Learn by Observing Others

AS we have seen, parents can strengthen good behavior patterns by arranging consequences that reward or reinforce the good behavior, and can alter bad behavior patterns by denying attention or providing unpleasant consequences when the child misbehaves. These principles have something in common: they change the way a child behaves by changing the way a parent reacts to his or her actions.

Another powerful influence on children's behavior occurs when a child watches others and then copies what he has seen them do. Because this phenomenon consists of an observer (the child) watching and copying the actions of someone else (the model), it is termed *modeling* or learning by imitation.

Parents have always known that children learn by watching others. At some time or other, most children dress up like their parents and copy things they have seen them do, such as getting ready for work, doing household chores, taking care of a baby (doll), and so on. Children will even pick up on unintentional mannerisms or nervous habits they have observed in a parent, often to the adult's embarrassment. When parents themselves misbehave, they often try to keep the child from modeling their wrong behavior by admonishing the child, "Do as I say, not as I do." This, incidentally, does not usually work. A child is much more likely to imitate an action he has seen in his parent than to heed the parent's instruction. Even though parents know that children learn by imitating others, few are aware of just how important this kind of learning can be and how strongly it influences a child's behavior.

LIKE PARENT, LIKE CHILD

Children often display many of the same characteristics, values, habits, interests, behavior patterns, and abilities their parents exhibit. Although some people have concluded that "like parent, like child" similarities mean that all these characteristics must be inherited, a more likely explanation is that parents serve as powerful early models for their children. Over time, children learn (both intentionally and unintentionally) to imitate the behavior they see in their parents.

Although parents are models for their children's behavior, they aren't the only models in the child's life. Children also learn to imitate actions they see in other adults (such as teachers or older brothers and sisters), other children (siblings or friends), and even fictional models (characters seen in television programs or movies, or characters in books).

Over the course of a child's development, the relative influence of these models changes. For example, parents are the primary models for children under the age of five. Later, as a child reaches school age, peers or friends and television characters rapidly gain in importance because the child now spends more time with these friends and is exposed to more television. Parents of school-age children almost always notice how quickly their youngsters develop the habits, mannerisms, language, and dress of their friends. They also see clear evidence of the behavioral copying of favorite TV characters in their child's play. In fact, during adolescence, peer models may become even more important than the family. Parents are frequently amazed and concerned to find that their adolescent suddenly has attitudes, habits, and preferences very different from theirs. This is a predictable and entirely normal part of development. Often a swing back to the values originally modeled by the parents occurs as adolescents reach adulthood.

Children obviously do not imitate all the actions they see exhibited by significant people in their lives, whether those models are parents, friends, brothers and sisters, or show-business personalities. In general, children are likely to imitate the conduct of models who are friendly, likable, and admired by the child; are of the same sex as the child; are seen as having interests and backgrounds similar to the child's; are the same age as (or older than) the child; and whose actions seem to pay off in ways that are attractive to the child.

Because parents, friends, and television characters are often observed by youngsters and meet most of these standards, they tend to become the most important influences on children's modeled learning.

HOW PARENTS SERVE AS GOOD (OR BAD) MODELS FOR THEIR CHILDREN

The process of learning through modeling is neither a good nor a bad process; it is simply one of the ways children acquire their behavior patterns. Whether a child's conduct will be improved or worsened depends on the actual behavior the child observes in other people. When children are exposed to models who exhibit undesirable behavior (such as swearing, sloppiness, aggression, dishonesty, or a nasty temper), it is likely that they will develop similar characteristics. Children who are routinely exposed to positive behavior (honesty, kindness, communicating or working out strategies for dealing with conflicts verbally rather than through aggression) tend to imitate these characteristics. Since parents are such important models in their children's lives, they should consider how their own actions can influence a child's behavior.

One of the cardinal rules for parents as models is simply not to be hypocritical. If a parent has the habit of swearing when he or she gets angry, sooner or later that parent's child is likely to do exactly the same thing and probably use the same words. Similarly, if a parent doesn't attach very much importance to doing routine, around-the-house chores, but then expects the child to do these things, there is an inconsistency between what the child sees the parent doing and the different behavior that is being requested of the child. In most cases parents can (and probably should) expect that their children will imitate the actions actually seen in the parent model.

While things like cursing and lack of neatness are relatively minor difficulties, more serious behavior problems can also be traced, in part, to a child's modeling experiences. Aggression is one. When children are exposed to models (including parents, friends, or televised characters) who consistently deal with conflicts by fighting, becoming angry, or behaving aggressively, the child's own likelihood of handling conflicts in just this manner will increase. Several studies have suggested that the problems of adults are sometimes traceable to earlier modeling experiences. For example, studies have shown that children who have been treated harshly (and even abusively) by their parents later tend to be punitive and harsh toward their own children. Also, studies of adult problem drinkers indicate that they had often been raised by parents who also drank abusively and excessively. Even the problem of obesity may have at least some roots in children's modeling experiences; a disproportionate number of overweight children have over-weight parents, suggesting that kids may observe and imitate overeating styles exhibited by significant models in their lives.

While these and other findings point to the important role of modeling in children's development, you need not be overly conscious about your parental behavior. A parent who becomes too self-conscious about everyday actions would generate more difficulties than there were in the first place. We all know some aggressive children with nonaggressive parents, overweight children whose parents are thin, and children who develop the habit of cursing when their parents never swear. Again, because parents are not the only people in a child's life, they are not the only models. Many behavior patterns are learned as a result of a child's own experience rather than by observation of others. We're only saying here that parents should be aware that children do learn by imitation and that it's therefore useful to model actions, values, and behavior styles consistent with those you want to see in your child.

THE EFFECTS OF TELEVISED VIOLENCE: WHAT PARENTS SHOULD KNOW

Recent studies have shown that the average person in this country watches more than six hours of television a day. When the time spent in movie theaters is added to this, it becomes evident that most children are exposed to heavy doses of the broadcast media. While your own child's TV watching may well be less than this national average, if your youngster is like most kids, he still sees a lot of television. During the past ten years, psychologists, parents, and broadcasters have been interested in the effects of televised violence on children. This interest largely developed when many television programs (including those shown during the afternoons and early evenings, and even the Saturday morning cartoons) were characterized by scenes depicting a great deal of violence and aggression. The question arose: Do children who watch violence on TV become more aggressive in their own behavior?

The answer is a qualified yes. A number of psychologists, among them Dr. Albert Bandura at Stanford University, have shown children films that include the kind of violence youngsters might really see on television. Children watched these violent films and were observed immediately afterward as they played with one another. The children who watched violent films were indeed much more aggressive in their play than children who had seen nonviolent films. In some cases children directly mimicked the acts of aggression (hitting, punching, yelling, pretending to shoot a gun) they had just seen on film. Later studies confirmed this conclusion and found that children will model and imitate not only the aggression they see exhibited by actors in televised programs but even the artificial aggressiveness of animated cartoon characters. Still another result of viewing violent films has been uncovered: Exposure to televised violence increases children's tolerance of aggressive and antisocial acts. In one study, children who at first said they felt that certain aggressive conduct was wrong were shown film models engaging in it. Afterward the children reported that the aggressive behavior wasn't really so bad. It appears that repeated exposure to modeled violence numbs a child to the fact that such conduct is wrong. These implications are sufficient to cause concern.

The effect on children of occasionally seeing aggression on their home TV sets is probably not quite as clear-cut. One factor that influences whether a child will actually imitate televised violence is the child's own level of aggression. Kids who are more aggressive, inclined to fight, and who behave violently have not yet really learned that these actions are wrong. They are therefore also the children most likely to be influenced by the further (and perhaps new methods of) violence they see on TV. Children with well-established and well-reinforced patterns of good behavior are less likely to be affected by something they see briefly on television or in a movie.

Over the past several years broadcasters claim to have reduced the amount of aggression depicted in television programs, especially those shown when children are most likely to be watching. Similarly, movies are rated (P, PG, R, or X) using a system that takes into account the amount of violence portrayed. Still, because watching media violence can influence a child's behavior and conduct standards, parents should follow some commonsense rules:

1. Young children in particular should not be permitted to watch shows or films with high aggressive content. Children under six have a limited range of experience and understanding

about what kind of behavior is right or wrong. Against this backdrop of limited personal experience, violence seen on television or in films may more strongly influence their own actions.

2. Children who are already prone to aggression or fighting shouldn't watch programs that will further reinforce this misbehavior pattern demonstrated by others.

3. Aggression in cartoons, although it seems unrealistic to adults, can still influence children. Cartoon characters who hit, punch, or kick each other, who throw other characters off buildings and cliffs, or who tie one another to railroad tracks, may seem silly and unrealistic to adults. But even this unreal kind of violence can influence a young child watching it. While cartoons have been made increasingly less violent, a parent should still monitor them for excess aggression.

4. Keep an eye on the cable. Cable television often airs films with violent content unsuitable for children (although they're usually shown later at night and are often preceded by parental guidance announcements). If you subscribe to pay television, you might want to check the suitability of a program for children.

If your child seems affected by violence he has seen, have a talk with him about it. If you notice your child imitating (or even talking about engaging in) an aggressive act he has seen in a media presentation, explain why the action is bad, the potential harm it could cause, and the unpleasant consequences you will institute if he does it. Then suggest to your youngster which actions might be more acceptable than using, say, a kung fu karate chop when he's mad at someone else.

MODELING: A POSITIVE TEACHING APPROACH

Up to this point we've talked about the potentially negative effects that can occur when children are consistently exposed to the misbehavior of others. But children also learn many desirable characteristics by observing them in other people, and the modeling process itself can serve a useful role in solving behavior problems. Just as children may imitate bad behavior they see, they also can be taught desirable new skills. A parent is in the position to create opportunities for his or her child to develop positive characteristics and to overcome existing behavior problems through modeling.

WATCH ME DO IT!

All children under the age of six have a limited ability to understand complicated verbal directions. This is normal; it simply takes time for a child's comprehension abilities to develop fully. Yet long before he can understand and follow detailed verbal direction, the child is able to copy or imitate fairly complicated actions he sees in others. You can take advantage of this fact by using modeling to show your child how to engage in actions you want to see him exhibit. Let's look at a common behavior problem — shyness — to see how imitating can help solve this difficulty.

Shyness. As toddlers start getting older, parents begin to occupy less of their time and playmates more. Although some children have little or no trouble developing friendships, joining in neighborhood group activities, and playing cooperatively, others do experience difficulties in this area. These difficulties may take the form of excessive shyness or loneliness, or they may show up in aggressive behavior and alienation of others. In either case, problems in getting along with other children often develop because the child has simply not yet mastered the skills needed to establish and maintain good friendships with other kids. These skills involve such things as walking up to and greeting others, knowing how to get yourself included in others' activities, inviting others to join in your own activities, and sharing. To the degree that a child has not learned to do such things, problems in peer relationships can occur.

It is not surprising that many children run into difficulties making and keeping friends. This is all a new area for the young child, one in which he or she initially has no personal experience. If a youngster has older brothers, sisters, or friends to serve as social models, he or she can imitate their conduct. When children don't have these models, peer relationship skills may be acquired more slowly. This is probably a major reason why shy children tend to come from families where there aren't outgoing older brothers, sisters, or close friends who can serve as natural models for the younger child.

If, for whatever reason, your child has not learned how to meet and get along with other children, you can create special learning experiences to teach him those skills. In our clinic we often make videotape films that show children doing those things that cause the shy child difficulty, such as playing with a group of kids on a playground or inviting children home after school. We ask that the shy youngster carefully watch the filmed models and then try to imitate what he or she sees them doing. In this way we use modeling to teach shy or withdrawn children the same skills that popular, outgoing kids use to make and keep friends. It is a direct and effective approach.

Parents, of course, don't have access to specially made films, but there are other ways to apply the same modeling principles with their children. Depending upon the age of the youngster and the kinds of situations in which he or she is shy, parents can:

- model, in play acting form, what *they* would say and do in specific situations the child finds difficult, and then let the child rehearse doing the same thing with them. In this way parents can show their children how to make friends, play games with others, and so on;

- arrange for the child to spend time with a special big-brother or big-sister chum who can also help teach the child skills for becoming more popular with others (such as games or sports skills);
- plan new activities that will bring the child into more contact with other children and thereby provide more positive opportunities for the youngster to observe others and practice his own social skills.

In chapter 9 we will discuss in more detail how parents can follow these steps if their child has difficulty getting along with others. The important point to bear in mind here is that being able to observe skilled models, when combined with opportunities for the child to then actually practice those skills in a warm and nonthreatening environment, is an approach that assists children in overcoming their shyness.

"Let's do it together": An effective way to encourage your child to follow directions. In the example we've just discussed, the principle of modeling desired conduct was applied to the rather specific problem of making friends. Modeling can also be used on an everyday basis to encourage your child to follow the directions you give or the requests you make.

Most of the time, when a parent wants a child to do something he or she just tells or asks the child to do it ("Clean up your room," "Why don't you go play with your toys?," "Go out and get your toys off the driveway," "Play with your sister until dinner"). Many parents feel they spend a lot of their time giving directions to their children. Even so, parents may find that their child doesn't follow those directions or requests. When we talked about ways to strengthen good behavior patterns, we stressed the importance of consistently reinforcing a child's desirable conduct. One way to improve your child's compliance with requests is by remembering to praise the youngster when he does follow a direction. "Pick up your toys" should be followed by praise, a thank-you, or some other recognition while the youngster is actually picking up those toys.

A second approach for improving your child's compliance makes use of the modeling principle. When a parent gives a child a direction, he is telling the youngster to do something in a one-way style of communication. Most of us resist being told what to do; we just don't like being the recipients of other people's one-way commands. Even though they are young, children don't always respond well to one-way directions either. A good alternative is to make tasks into activities that parent and child can team up and do together. For example, let's assume that Mr. Smith wants his five-year-old son Bobby to gather up some pieces of paper and crayons from the living-room floor after the boy has finished playing with them. Bobby, however, is now watching TV. The one-way approach a parent might take in the situation could sound like this:

Mr. Smith: "Bobby, you need to pick up the crayons and papers in the living room."

Bobby: (No reply because he is watching TV.)

Mr. Smith: "Bobby, you need to get this cleaned up; when you finish playing with things you need to put them away."

Bobby: "Uh-huh" (but still no real response).

Mr. Smith: (After a few minutes) "Bobby, I gave you a direction. I want you to listen to me."

Bobby: "OK, I'll do it in a minute."

Mr. Smith: "Not in a minute. If you don't listen to me, you're going to be in trouble.

It isn't hard to see that this interaction isn't working very well. Probably the father will eventually raise his voice, show anger, and only then, when Bobby knows his father is really serious, will the youngster go to pick up his things.

But there's another way. Instead of telling Bobby to go pick up his crayons, the parent could make the responsibility a shared one: "Bobby, it's time to get the living room picked up. Things need to get put away when you're done with them. C'mon, we'll do it together and it'll be finished in a minute. Then we'll watch the TV show" (taking the child by the hand, the parent leads him into the living room). Here the parent is moving away from the practice of dispensing one-way commands and instead is making the problem a task that he helps the child accomplish.

Why is this approach effective? Remember the notion of modeling. If children acquire behavior patterns by seeing them in others, then it will be more effective for a parent to model desirable conduct by participating in tasks with a child rather than by telling a child to do those tasks. The child should not passively watch as the parent does all the chores intended to be the child's responsibilities, of course. However, by teaming up with your child to do things, you will be modeling the exact conduct you expect from the child, you'll be able to avoid feeling like a continual direction-giver, and your child will probably find the chores much more enjoyable because he's now part of a team effort. Working together in this way also permits the parent to see and praise the child's efforts while they are taking place, providing further incentive for the child to behave well and pitch in.

MODELING GOOD BEHAVIOR: SHOW IN ADDITION TO TELL

Although it is reasonable for parents to be sensitive to the fact that children can learn misbehavior patterns by observing them in others, it is even more important that they keep in mind that children are able to acquire positive habits in the same way. It is often easier and more effective for parents to model those actions they would like to see strengthened. As we now turn our attention to solving specific behavior problems, we will also see how modeling can be a positive part of those solutions.

5/
Solving the Problems of Aggression, Noncompliance, and Tantrums

IN our own child clinic and probably in most others, parents frequently report that their children are hard to control. In some youngsters this takes the form of talking back and refusing to follow parents' directions. In other cases the child's conduct may be more physically aggressive and include throwing tantrums or out-and-out fighting.

Children's anger-related behavior problems are especially frustrating to parents for several reasons. One, of course, is that the child is misbehaving in a way that is hard to ignore and directly challenges the parent's feelings of authority. But perhaps even more important, when parents do act to deal with their child's aggressive or noncompliant behavior, they often find themselves doing things that they as parents can't feel very good about. Scolding, spanking, screaming at a child — all of these are last-ditch responses that may hurt and upset the parent just as much as (or more than) the misbehaving child. So, while tantrumming and noncompliance, certainly don't fit the ideal that most parents have in mind for their child's conduct, the parent forced into using unpleasant threats and actions to control those problems can also be left feeling frustrated, guilty, and upset at his own behavior. That's why it is important for the well-being of both child and parent to develop new ways of handling anger-related behavior problems.

The approaches to behavior problems we will cover in this chapter have three features in common. First, they require little or no physical punishment, such as spanking. This may surprise some parents, especially those who on their own have found few alternatives to spanking as a routine form of discipline. Second, the approaches we will outline do provide some negative consequences when the child behaves unacceptably. This is necessary to reduce the child's misbehavior, but it can be done in a nonviolent way that parents will not have to feel guilty about. Third, we want to use approaches that will teach children more acceptable actions to replace those current ones that cannot be tolerated.

This latter point is a critical one that deserves closer attention. In the majority of cases, children act out in angry, aggressive, or noncompliant ways when they are frustrated about something. The situation might be a parent's simple and reasonable request that the child stop doing something he finds enjoyable ("OK. That's enough TV for tonight because it's time to go to bed"), or it could be a request that the child start doing something he doesn't want to do ("Get ready because you have to be at the doctor's office at 3:00"). Either of these events can provoke a tantrum. Similar problems occur when the child's wishes are in conflict with those of another child ("I hit him because he tried to change the channel while I was watching television"). You as a parent probably have a good idea of which particular situations, frustrations, and conflicts can trigger your own child to act out.

To solve these anger-related difficulties, we do want to bring an end to such things as tantrums, talking back, fighting, or destructiveness because they are unacceptable actions. On the other hand, we don't want the child to become a passive, compliant individual who feels it is a punishable offense merely to express his or her own opinions, preferences, and viewpoints. Our overall aim will thus be to reduce the child's more aggressive displays of temper while at the same time encouraging him to express his feelings in a more constructive, acceptable manner.

Encouraging your child to talk about feelings (including feelings of displeasure or anger) will work only if you as a parent are really willing to discuss your child's viewpoints. This may involve changing how you react when your child disagrees with you or asks why you made a certain request of him. It is important for children to develop the ability to express their own views, provided the dialogue is handled calmly and not in an angry fashion. Such an exchange gives you an opportunity to explain the reasons for decisions you make and in turn fosters your child's ability to convey emotions in an appropriate manner.

This is a crucial skill for children and adults to acquire. All of us are capable of being angered or upset by situations in our lives, including fairly minor everyday frustrations similar to those that can provoke children's tantrums. There are times when adults really do want to yell, scream, cry, break something, or hit someone. Most of the time, though, we don't do these things because we've learned that it is better (if a bit less satisfying) to assert our feelings in a more calm, verbal manner. That is the same kind of maturity we want to foster in children who currently have anger-related behavior problems. The techniques we will now describe bring about this kind of behavior change.

HOW TO HANDLE TANTRUMS

It is a rare child who does not throw tantrums at least on an occasional basis. When your child does have an outburst of crying, screaming, or even hitting, he is probably doing it for two reasons. One is that the child is angry, either at you or at some other circumstance that is in conflict with what he wants, and he wants to convey his anger. The second reason, one that develops over time, is that children of four, five, or six learn they may actually be able to get what they want by tantrumming. To the extent that parents give in to tantrums (thereby rewarding them), children are apt to tantrum frequently as a way to get things from adults. In essence the child becomes able to dictate what the parents will do by having a tantrum.

WHEN DOES YOUR CHILD THROW TANTRUMS?

Most kids who have temper problems throw their tantrums somewhat predictably; parents almost know ahead of time when a tantrum is most likely to happen. In our clinic we see children who will regularly tantrum before school (or in the car on the way to school), when told it is time for bed, or, most common of all, when told by their parents they have to do something they don't want to do. The first step a parent should take to solve the problem of temper tantrums is to determine when the child is most likely to resort to them. To do this, think back over the past week or several weeks and see whether you can recall just when, where, and in what situations your child threw tantrums:

- Are they most likely to happen at home, at school, or in some other public place (such as at a store, in a car, at a restaurant, or at a relative's house)?
- Do tantrums occur at any special time of the day?
- Do tantrums occur more often with one parent, both parents, or neither parent present? Do both parents handle tantrums in the same way?
- What has triggered the tantrums the child has thrown over the past week or two? Do they happen in response to some particular conflict situation or when the child is frustrated in a certain way?
- What have you done to handle each of these tantrums? Did you ignore them, spank or scold the child, back down from what you wanted, try to reason with the angry child, or did you handle tantrums in different ways depending on the occasion?

Thinking carefully about when your child tantrums will help you plan how to handle the problem. As we'll see, tantrums that take place at the grocery store must be handled differently, for practical reasons, from those occurring at home. Some children tend to throw more tantrums with one person (such as their mother or a grandparent) than with others. This tells us that it will be important for all the adults in the child's family to start handling temper tantrums in the same manner, so the child learns that these misbehaviors will be dealt with consistently. And if a parent handles tantrums in inconsistent ways (ignoring on some occasions, spanking on others, and giving in at still others times), we'll also want to reduce this inconsistency so the child learns that the same consequence will always happen whenever and wherever tantrums are thrown.

STEP ONE: DISCUSS WITH YOUR CHILD WHY TANTRUMS ARE UNACCEPTABLE (AND WHAT TO DO INSTEAD OF TANTRUMMING)

If your child is old enough to understand a discussion of his behavior (usually around the age of three), you can begin to solve tantrum problems by talking with the child about them. Pick a quiet time when you can sit down with your child to discuss your concerns about his or her tantrumming. The time you select should not be in the midst of a problem situation and it should never be when you are angry with the child. An evening when things are calm is an ideal time for this discussion. We recommend that the discussion include both parents (if yours is a two-parent family) as well as the child, or children, who have the tantrum problem.

Begin your discussion by calmly explaining to the child that tantrums are bad and will no longer be permitted because they disrupt the family, cause unpleasantness to everyone involved, and because the child is now old enough to stop throwing tan-

trums when he or she is angry. Then explain that you understand that the child may sometimes get angry or upset by
things, and mention specifically several recent situations in
which the youngster did throw a tantrum. As you do this, tell
the child what specific actions he could have taken in those
situations instead of tantrumming. Make it clear to the child
that it is fine for him to tell you when he is angry or disagrees
with a decision you've made, and let the child know that you
will really listen to his wishes or disagreements (and you won't
be angry with him) if he tells you about his feelings. In short,
discuss with your child how people can convey feelings in ways
other than angry outbursts. Provide specific examples of how to
do this. Remember to gear the level of your discussion to your
child's ability to understand; if the child is only three or four,
keep your discussion simple and direct.

For children who are five or six, you can also use modeling
to teach alternatives to tantrums. By modeling we mean here
that you will show the child what he should say instead of
throwing a tantrum. Refer again to one of the recent situations
that provoked a tantrum and model for your child what he
could have said to you in that situation. For example, let's
assume your child threw a tantrum one night last week when
told it was time for bed. In your discussion, recall this situation
and model what the child could have told you by saying out
loud: "Mom, I'm watching TV. If I get all ready for bed right
now, can I stay up a half hour later to watch it?" Or, if your
child threw a tantrum last week right before a dentist appointment, show your child what he might have said in place of
having that tantrum: "I don't *want* to go to the dentist. It'll
hurt and I don't want to go." After you have modeled several
examples and you think he knows how to express his feelings
verbally, tell the youngster that if he expresses his dislikes to
you by talking them out you'll be very pleased with him. Also
say that if possible you will be willing to try to work out some
compromise in the conflict situation. Even if it turns out that

you can't compromise, tell your child that you will always be glad to discuss his feelings when he conveys them to you without tantrumming.

STEP TWO: TIME-OUT FOR TANTRUMS

After you've had this discussion with your child, and even if it seemed to go well, don't expect that tantrum problems will automatically disappear. Remember, children learn from the consequences of their actions, not merely by talking about a difficulty you are having with their behavior. So, you will want to establish actual learning experiences that encourage your child to reduce how often he tantrums and to increase his more acceptable behavior.

Brief time-out is one of the most effective techniques for tantrums; it should replace the other disciplines you have previously used for tantrumming. If in the past you have spanked, scolded, ignored, or just given in to tantrums, stop doing these things and begin using the time-out technique we described in chapter 3. Consistency in using time-out after each tantrum is why it is an effective solution. Return now to chapter 3 and read the time-out section once again. Read carefully, because you will need to follow this procedure quite closely when your child tantrums. Decide where your time-out location will be, making certain that it fits the guidelines we discussed, and have the kitchen timer handy.

When your child first starts to tantrum, instruct him once to stop his tantrum and tell him that time-out will have to follow unless he does so. Right after you've done this, calmly ask if the child would be willing to talk with you about whatever is angering him. This is an invitation for the child to express himself verbally — something we want to encourage. If the youngster does accept your invitation to calm down and say what he's feeling without tantrumming, praise the child for doing this and discuss what the child feels, what your position is, and whether or not you are able to compromise with him. Don't become defensive because your child is asserting his feelings at this point, provided he does it reasonably. Even if you cannot work out a compromise to the conflict, let the child know that you are pleased that he is offering his opinions and views without temper outbursts.

It would be ideal if your child did stop a tantrum before it began and discussed his feelings with you calmly. It won't always happen. If your child does not repond to your suggestion to talk about his feelings and if he continues to tantrum after you've made this suggestion, immediately use time-out:

- The child is to go to the time-out location;
- There is no further discussion about anything once you've told the child to go to time-out;
- Time-out lasts five minutes (for children under five years old) or one minute per year of age for children over five. This is the amount of time the child spends quietly in time-out;
- Refusal to go to time-out, or continued tantrumming while in time-out, are dealt with exactly in the ways described in chapter 3;
- When the timer rings, signaling the end of time-out, the discipline is over and no further punishment takes place;
- If your child intentionally broke or destroyed something during the tantrum, have him rearrange anything that was thrown or repair any damage. If the youngster is not old enough to do this, at least require him to help you straighten things up.

What should I do when my child throws tantrums away from home? The basic time-out system we have outlined works well for temper tantrums occurring at home and near the time-out location. Unfortunately, children's tantrums don't always take place where they can be most easily handled. Children throw tantrums in the grocery store, in restaurants, in the car, at the shopping mall, and at their grandparents' house. Parents sometimes get the feeling their children intentionally have tantrums in places where the parent will encounter the greatest difficulty and embarrassment in trying to stop them.

If your child has tantrums at someone else's house, and if the someone else is a close relative or a trusted person who often cares for your child, tantrums should be handled in exactly the same manner as if they were occurring in your home. This will entail teaching grandmother or Aunt Sally how to use time-out correctly, as well as how to recognize and reinforce the child's control of anger and good behavior efforts. The techniques we are discussing will be equally effective whether the parent or some other relative is using them, so long as they are followed correctly and carefully. In fact, we frequently find in our clinic that a child's behavior improves at home when the parents start using time-out but does not improve at relatives' homes until they also handle tantrums the same way.

Tantrums that take place in public places must be handled a bit differently, since time-out cannot be carried out in stores, restaurants, or similar locations. If tantrums develop away from home, tell your child that unless he stops tantrumming he will have to go to time-out as soon as you get home. If the tantrum continues beyond this one warning, the child should be firmly but calmly told you will need to add five minutes to the basic time-out period once he gets home. If necessary, repeat this "five more minutes" extension up to two times, so the child will have to spend as much as ten minutes in addition to the basic time-out period once he does get home. Again, never exceed a total of thirty minutes in time-out and use the five-minute-more strategy only if the child disregards your first warning.

Continue your activities even if your child has tantrummed away from home — it's important that your child not dictate through tantrums what you will (or won't) be able to do. As soon as you get home, however, the child must immediately go to time-out as a consequence for the tantrum thrown earlier. Time-out is used even if the child's behavior improved after the tantrumming episode. As your child goes to time-out, give him or her a brief reminder about why this is happening ("Todd, you're going to time-out now because you threw that tantrum at Kroger's and I told you that you'd have to go to time-out for it"). Always handle away-from-home tantrums in exactly this way.

STEP THREE: REWARD YOUR CHILD'S GOOD BEHAVIOR

Time-out is only one part of the solution to tantrum problems. While all tantrums should be followed by time-out, we still want to strengthen your child's good behavior. There are several ways to do this. Continue to have periodic discussions with your child focusing on ways to express wishes without tantrumming. Earlier we suggested that parents begin their efforts to solve tantrum problems with a discussion in which the parent models what the child could have said in situations when he tantrummed. For children with frequent tantrumming problems, these discussions can be repeated regularly once or twice a week. Your aim here is to actively teach your child ways to express feelings by talking, and to encourage the child to then use these talking skills in situations where he formerly threw tantrums. If your child is under five, give some direct and simple examples of what he should do in situations where tantrums take place (such as "Timmy, I don't want you to scream and yell when you are mad. Tell me what you want, instead."). If your youngster is over five, you can practice alternatives to tantrumming. Model examples of what the child could have said, and use as your examples some of the situations in which tantrums actually took place. Then ask your child to pretend he is in the situation in which he previously tantrummed, but now have the child repeat the same kind of expression of feelings you just modeled. As he does this, offer your praise and let him know, clearly and convincingly, how happy you will be when he expresses his feelings by talking, because that's the way grown-ups resolve their disagreements.

Notice — and reinforce — occasions when your child does not tantrum. After using time-out for tantrums and the practice sessions in which you teach your child alternatives to throwing tantrums, you will gradually start to see some indications that the child is controlling his or her temper. Whenever your child starts to get angry but then tells you what is bothering him instead, recognize this improved behavior and immediately praise him for it (and, of course, then try to resolve the conflict once the child lets his feelings be known). Also be observant of occasions when your child could have thrown a tantrum but didn't. For example, a youngster might typically have tantrums at bedtime, at schooltime, or when asked not to do something. When one of these situations passes without an eruption, be sure to notice it and tell your child you are pleased he acted so well. Provide plenty of extra recognition for your child's behavior in situations where outbursts are no longer occurring as often as in the past, even if you still have to use time-out on some occasions. Combine time-out for tantrums that do happen with praise for tantrums that didn't happen.

Prevent tantrums by rewarding good behavior in situations that formerly provoked tantrums. We have discussed the general strategy of reinforcing a behavior that is the opposite of the action we want to see decreased. This approach can be used to actually prevent tantrums. Parents often know when their child will throw a tantrum. If you can see the possibility of a tantrum coming, you are also in a position to prevent it by developing a plan to reward the child for controlling his tantrumming. For example, let's suppose that a young child frequently tantrums when she goes with her mother to the grocery store. The parent can set up a reward system whereby the child can earn something she wants after the trip (perhaps a treat from the checkout counter, coupled with praise), but only if she did not tantrum in the store. In essence the parent is establishing a good-behavior game to reinforce the absence of tantrumming in a specific situation where that misbehavior previously occurred. This approach works best if the child is old enough (usually about five) to understand exactly what he or she will need to do to earn the reward, and if the situation in which good behavior is expected is clearly identified ahead of time. For kids under five, rely on immediate praise to reinforce improved behavior.

Although tantrums are among the most upsetting behavior problems to parents, combining time-out with very active efforts to teach and reinforce better behavior in the child is a strategy that works well in most cases. The two most important aspects of solving tantrum behavior problems are your consistency in following tantrums with brief time-outs and your remaining highly attentive to occasions when the child behaves well so that you can reinforce his or her good behavior.

HOW TO HANDLE NONCOMPLIANCE

Noncompliance is the term we use when a child refuses to follow reasonable requests or directions given by the parent. A child's noncompliance may be passive, meaning the child simply doesn't pay attention and ignores what is being requested, or it may be more active, with the child actually saying that he or she won't do something you ask. Parents find both kinds of noncompliance very frustrating. In addition, events that started off as small instances of noncompliance can easily escalate into major power struggles between a parent and child. Usually this power struggle develops when the parent reacts to the child's refusal to follow a direction by trying to force or threaten the child into compliance. As the child continues to balk and as the parent becomes more angry, what started off as a routine request can become a major test of control that often ends in spanking.

Earlier we noted that a common mistake made by many parents is trying to force the child into doing something good by threatening him with something bad. This motivating-through-threats strategy often leads to trouble. One problem is that a parent will have to spend a great deal of time threatening, nagging, and actually punishing the child for not doing what is being requested. Another problem is that the parent, finding this whole pattern unpleasant, won't want to discipline repeated noncompliance and will simply stop expecting things of the child.

There's an easier way, one in which your child will actually come to seek out opportunities to do things he currently refuses to do.

STEP ONE: KEEP NOTES ON YOUR CHILD'S NONCOMPLIANCE FOR ONE WEEK

In order to gain more specific information about your child's noncompliance, we suggest you keep a little diary listing all the occasions when you have asked your child to do something and the child has not followed your request. This record sheet will serve as the basis for a Good-Behavior Game that we will describe later. In this diary the parent simply makes a brief notation for each noncompliance incident, mentioning (1) what was asked of the child, (2) what the child did, and (3) what the parent did to handle the situation. We suggest you keep such a sheet handy so you can record situations immediately after they occur. Don't tell your child you are keeping this record, which is for your information only. Keep the diary for one week, recording all instances of noncompliance.

STEP TWO: AFTER THE WEEK IS OVER, REVIEW YOUR
SHEET TO PINPOINT AREAS OF NONCOMPLIANCE

Children are usually noncompliant about things they don't like to do. A child who doesn't like to do homework will balk at parental requests to do schoolwork, a child who doesn't enjoy picking up her room will ignore requests to keep it straightened, and a child who doesn't want to go to bed will try to avoid it. It's human nature to disregard requests to do things we'd prefer not to do. To pinpoint areas of noncompliance for your own child, review the diary you kept over the week. Certain kinds of requests probably tend to be ignored or rejected by your child. What sorts of things would you like to see your child do, on his own, so you will not have to nag him? See whether you can identify situations or tasks about which your child is now noncompliant. You can use this information to develop a plan that encourages your child to do these things on his own.

STEP THREE: START THE GOOD-BEHAVIOR GAME
WITH YOUR CHILD

The Good-Behavior Game is an approach that motivates children without constant reminders from their parents. It is most effective for youngsters over five years old. (If your child is under five, the Good-Behavior Game is probably too complex and you should instead use the approaches for three- to five-year-olds we will discuss shortly.) Begin by selecting from your diary an activity that your child won't now do on his own — taking a bath, putting dirty clothes in the hamper, picking up toys after playtime, or taking care of a pet. Although you may find several different areas of noncompliance, focus on only one in the Good-Behavior Game. When that problem is successfully overcome you can move on to another activity.

Next, make up a Good-Behavior Game chart. The chart

can be a large calender or a hand-drawn chart with at least seven boxes, one for each day of the week. The boxes should be large enough that you can mark big stars in them. You might also want to put a title on the chart (like "Donald's a Good Boy for Helping Mom!") and a little drawing to symbolize the activity you are focusing on in the Good-Behavior Game. For example, if you want your child to pick up his toys, draw a few toys somewhere on the chart.

Explain to your child that you are going to begin a game in which he can earn something special by doing, with just one reminder from you, the activity that now elicits noncompliance. If picking up play toys is the issue, explain exactly what you mean by picking them up. Whatever behavior you choose to include in the Good-Behavior Game, explain clearly what is expected and tell the child that you will only remind him to do it once. If he does not follow your one request within five minutes he loses that day's game. Tape the chart in a visible location, such as on the refrigerator door or in your child's bedroom.

When the game goes into effect, your child's challenge is to carry out the selected responsibility when you ask him to. When he does follow your request, you also have several responsibilities. These are immediately praising your child for following your request, proudly marking a big star in the chart's box for that day, and rewarding your child with some special privilege. As we saw in chapter 2, tangible privileges might include things like a later-than-usual bedtime, some special activity he enjoys, a small allowance, and so on. The reinforcer you use should be one your youngster enjoys and will work to earn. We often advise parents to let their child help pick out the special reward or privilege that can be earned in the Good-Behavior Game.

What should you do if your child doesn't win the game one day? This will probably happen at some point, and you should handle it by simply explaining that because he didn't follow your request, he won't get the star or special reward. Encourage him or her to do better the next day. If you use privilege incentives that the youngster really enjoys, and if you couple these with plenty of praise and positive recognition for the child's success, the Good-Behavior Game can be used to solve many behavior problems of children over five.

There are two limitations of the game, however. It can be applied to only one problem at a time, and it works best for children over five. There are some other strategies that parents can use to reduce the noncompliance of children, including youngsters too young for the Good-Behavior Game.

HOW YOU MAKE REQUESTS OF YOUR CHILD DETERMINES WHETHER THEY WILL BE FOLLOWED

Parents who tell their child what to do (or not do) by issuing cold, short commands tend to have those commands ignored. "Go outside to play," "Clean up your room," "Do your homework," "Stop teasing the dog," or "Finish your sandwich" are all rapid-fire directions that children can easily resent and ignore. If you don't believe people respond badly to curt directions, think of those times when others in your life have barked directions at you. When you were the recipient of cold do and don't directions you probably resented it and felt annoyed at the person issuing those directions. Kids can feel the same thing.

Try this instead. When you want your child to do something (or to stop doing something), pretend you are talking to an adult you respect rather than to your child. Don't just give a direction, but instead tell your child in a warm, attentive manner that you'd appreciate it if he would do something differently. Then, give your child a reason for your direction so that he or she understands why you are making the request. Both these approaches will increase the likelihood that your child will listen to you and follow your direction. Here are several examples of bad versus good ways to give the same basic direction:

Bad Direction	Good Direction
"Stop teasing the dog."	"Johnny, I want you to stop teasing the dog. The reason is he'll get mad and bite you, so stop right now. Pet him nicely instead."
"Finish your sandwich."	"Susan, we'll all be late getting to the show if you don't finish up soon. You don't want that, so please finish eating your sandwich."
"Sit down."	"Tommy, I'd like you to stay in your seat until we're done eating. If you run around the restaurant people will get mad, so please sit down for a minute."

There's a very real difference in tone between the quick, cold direction and the better alternative, even though they are both requesting the same thing of the child. When children receive warm, encouraging directions that also include a brief reason for the request there is much stronger pull for them to comply. When requests are made of children in this more adult manner, parents tend to be rewarded with more adult behavior from their kids. Try this change of style with your own child.

GIVING DIRECTIONS IS ONLY HALF A PARENT'S TASK; THE OTHER CRITICAL HALF IS NOTICING AND REINFORCING COMPLIANCE WITH YOUR DIRECTION

The reward principle we've discussed throughout this book tells us that people do things that lead to positive outcomes for them and stop doing things that don't lead to recognition.

If children are asked by their parents to do something good (or asked to stop doing something bad), and if parents then neglect to positively recognize children's efforts, we can safely predict that children will soon stop following parental requests. The Good-Behavior Game is a structured way to reinforce one desirable conduct at a time. There are many other everyday occasions, however, when parents make routine requests of children that are not part of any formal Good-Behavior Game. Here it is equally important to actively reinforce compliance with these routine directions.

The easiest way to do this is simply by remembering to thank your child when he does something you just asked of him. Make certain you notice when your child follows a request you have given and then make certain the child knows you noticed it by praising, by thanking him, or by giving him a warm touch of your hand. The exact way you convey to the child that you noticed and appreciated his compliance is not critical; what is critical is that you provide positive and immediate attention and that you tell the child why you are happy with his behavior. For example, you might say to a little girl who just stopped banging a spoon against the table, "Tina, thank you for putting the spoon down when Mommy asked you to stop. You're such a good girl!" Children of all ages respond well to this kind of positive feedback.

REDIRECT YOUR CHILD TO A DESIRED BEHAVIOR

Telling a child "don't do that" or "stop doing that" conveys only that you are displeased with his current behavior; it doesn't tell the child what you'd like to see him or her doing instead. A more effective strategy is to redirect the child into behaving well. You can do this by following any request that a child stop doing something bad with a specific positive suggestion for what the child can do. Here's what we mean:

| To a child about to crayon on a wall: | "Mary, please don't mark on the wall. It won't come off. Here's a piece of paper to color on instead." |
| To a child bouncing a basketball off a wall near a window: | "Jimmy, don't do that. The ball can break the window. Go to the backyard and use the basketball hoop instead of the wall." |

Once the child has complied with your request, praise or thank the child for doing what you asked. That way you not only redirect your child into better behavior but you also reinforce the child's following your suggestion.

6/

Improving Your
Child's Self-Control

ONE of the major tasks all children face is the development of self-control. By self-control we mean the process by which children learn to delay or forestall some gratification because they are setting more mature, responsible standards for their own behavior. In essence the child is learning to resist doing what used to be very easy or enjoyable, and in its place the child is learning to behave in a more independent, responsible, and self-reliant manner. When parents take pride because their child is "growing up," they are usually referring to evidence of the child's increasing self-control.

Actually, the term "self-control" is somewhat misleading because it implies that children somehow develop the capacity to behave maturely and responsibly on their own. They do not. For a child to exercise internal self-control over his behavior, it is first necessary for that child to have been exposed to outside support, encouragement, and reinforcement for the actions the child needs to learn. Ordinarily, the source of this encouragement is the parents or some other adult.

In this chapter we will discuss several self-control issues common among young children. Even after the toilet training period, many youngsters continue to have occasional accidents; we will describe how parents can handle these mistakes. As we'll see, bed-wetting is another self-control problem that often confronts parents of a child under six. Children's curiosity about sex may also be an issue for parents at this time. While sexuality itself is hardly a behavior or self-control "problem," many parents don't know how to respond to their child's questions about sex or, even more often, how to handle their child's sex play. Since sexual feelings occur naturally in childhood and because parents may be uncertain how to teach children appropriate ways to express sexual interest, we will discuss the issue in this chapter. Finally, as youngsters reach the age of five or six they become capable of doing more things for themselves, things such as getting ready for day-care or school, and getting ready for bed. Parents often become frustrated by the minor but still troublesome problem of dawdling. Helping children overcome dawdling is the final growing-up issue we will describe in this chapter.

HOW TO HANDLE ACCIDENTS AFTER YOUR CHILD IS TOILET TRAINED

During early life, children learn that it is necessary to make all sorts of compromises with the world, giving up behavior patterns that have been very enjoyable and easy for more difficult, mature actions. Thus, as infants become children they learn that they will have to eat on a certain schedule, go to bed at a certain time, and get parental attention at times when the parent can provide it. One of the major self-control tasks in early childhood is learning to use the toilet. For most children, toilet training is accomplished sometime before the age of two; twenty months is an average age for initial training. Variability in readiness for training is natural, with some children able to master toilet use a bit earlier (and others a bit later) than this two-year average age.

Because we are focusing on children three years and older who are usually past the age of initial training, and because toilet training isn't really a behavior "problem" as such, we won't detail standard toilet training procedures here. Instead, we will consider how parents can best handle the mistakes or setbacks of youngsters who have already been trained. (If your child is not yet toilet trained you may wish to consult one of the special guides on this topic listed in the chapter 6 reference section at the end of the book.)

Parents — especially first-time parents — often underestimate the length of time required for children to reliably and consistently master toilet use. Even though a child may grasp the basics of using the bathroom at the age of two, it is not uncommon for three-, four-, and five-year-olds to experience occasional daytime accidents. Rather than causing alarm or anxiety, these periodic setbacks can be viewed by the parent as a normal part of the way children master complex new skills. We don't expect someone who has just learned to ride a bike never to fall off, nor should we be alarmed when the toilet-trained youngster has a wetting episode. On the other hand, when a child reaches the age when most of his playmates are dry, accidents can cause embarrassment and feelings of poor self-control. For this reason it is wise for parents of children over three to develop a plan that gently encourages greater self-control while avoiding practices that can create a sense of shame or failure in the child. Let's look at some ways to encourage better toilet use in children who have already been trained.

FIRST, SEE WHETHER YOU CAN ANALYZE WHEN YOUR CHILD HAS ACCIDENTS

Mrs. Hudson brought five-year-old Craig to our clinic because he seemed to forget when to use the toilet. Craig was first toilet trained at the age of two, but he had experienced occasional day-time wetting periods since then. Now, just before he was to start school, there was one accident nearly every day. Mrs. Hudson was concerned that Craig would be teased by his new schoolmates about the problem.

When Mrs. Hudson first consulted us, we asked her to take Craig to the family doctor for a check-up to rule out any medical cause, such as a urinary infection, for the problem. We recommend this to parents as a preliminary step because on rare occasions, medical conditions can be responsible for a child's daytime accidents. With medical causes ruled out, our next task was to help Mrs. Hudson analyze exactly when Craig's mistakes occurred. Pants-wetting often happens at fairly regular and predictable times; if we can discover what those times are, we can then develop a plan focused on those periods. For one week Mrs. Hudson observed Craig to see when these accidents took place. We asked her to record each day, on a piece of paper, (1) whether there were any such episodes, (2) at what time the pants became wet, (3) what Craig was doing immediately before the accident; and (4) how the mother handled the episode. Although Mrs. Hudson did not at first think there would be any pattern to Craig's problem, her week's records told a different story: Craig almost always had wet pants following periods of active play in the afternoon. To solve the problem, we needed to direct our attention to his toilet use before, during, or after periods of active play because this was when Craig forgot to use the bathroom.

To begin solving this problem with your child, keep the same kind of record Mrs. Hudson did. Pay particular attention to the time of day and child activities that seem to precede accidents. Intensive play was the activity that preceded Craig's wetting, but other common activities include the one-hour period following a child's intake of fluids; the time immediately following naps; occasions when the child is away from home and not near a familiar bathroom; and while the child is intently watching TV or otherwise deeply involved in some activity. Even if you cannot pin down a specific activity, at least try to determine the time of day when toilet use mistakes are most likely to happen. As you become able to predict when an accident is apt to occur, you are in a better position to solve the problem.

NEXT, PLAN FREQUENT BATHROOM USE PERIODS AROUND THOSE CRITICAL TIMES

The best way to help a child overcome pants-wetting is by ensuring that the youngster remembers to use the bathroom before, during, and after those periods when problems most often happen. If late afternoon is the problem time, your child should use the bathroom more often during late afternoon hours. Because Craig often had wet pants when he came in from playing outside, we asked Mrs. Hudson to make sure he always used the bathroom before going out to play and that he came in at half-hour intervals during his play time. A good rule of thumb is to have your youngster use the bathroom at least once an hour during the time of day you have identified as problematic. If you should ever sense that your child needs to use the bathroom (by noticing squirming, leg-wiggling or facial expressions), remind him to do so promptly.

There are two different ways to handle bathroom use. One is to have the child sit on the toilet once every hour throughout the high-risk time period, or before and during activities that now trigger accidents. We usually recommend this for children of three and for children who don't seem able to tell when they need to use the bathroom. If you do this, remain close enough to notice when your child urinates so you can praise him and let him leave the bathroom when he's through. Or you may simply want to ask your child whether he needs to use the bathroom on this more frequent-than-usual schedule rather than actually requiring him to sit on the toilet each time. If this reminder-only approach works, use it.

REINFORCEMENT FOR TOILET USE AND TAKING RESPONSIBILITY FOR WET PANTS

When your youngster does urinate in the toilet during these extra sessions, provide plenty of praise. Let your child know that you are pleased he uses the bathroom rather than his pants, and remind your child to use the bathroom on his own whenever he needs to. This is a good time to point out that he should stop playing, watching TV, or engaging in other high-risk activity as soon as he needs to use the toilet. Be especially alert to occasions when your child does go to the bathroom on his or her own without your reminder or questioning. Since this is the self-control behavior we really want to encourage, it is important to praise and recognize a youngster's spontaneous toilet use. If the child sits on the toilet and doesn't urinate, you must rely on your judgment to tell you what to do. If you think he doesn't need to use the bathroom then, just remind him to go to it when he senses the need. Should an accident happen shortly afterward, you will know that your child must sit on the toilet a little longer next time.

While your praise helps to motivate better self-control, you should also require the child to accept some responsibility for cleaning up after an accident. (The attention of being cleaned up and having new clothes put on may actually help to reinforce the problem.) As much as possible, given your child's age and manual ability to take off and put on clothes, have the child clean and change himself. Changing out of wet clothes should become the child's responsibility, even if you have to oversee and help him a bit.

Never belittle or shame your child for accidents. This only makes a child feel guilty and does little to solve the problem. Instead, rely on positive attention for correct bathroom use during the time of day your child is likely to have wet pants, and on increased responsibility for clothes changing following mistakes. It is also desirable to develop a special reward plan of the type we discussed in chapter 2 for days when no episodes occur.

When your child's toilet-use pattern improves, you can develop the habit of simply asking whether the child wants to use the bathroom during formerly risky periods (after naps, before playing, before going outside, and so on). As you notice continued improvement and as accidents become more rare, be sure to convey your pride that the child is doing so much better. Your child will probably feel more grown-up and confident when he hears that you're noticing — and proud of — the change.

This approach to toilet-use problems is effective for most children we see. Occasionally, however, the difficulty requires more specialized attention. If the problem does not improve within several months, outside advice may be needed.

HOW TO HANDLE BED-WETTING

Daytime accidents and nighttime bed-wetting are similar problems because in each case the child is not using the bathroom when he or she should. Just as our approach to accidents involved strengthening better toilet-use patterns, our general approach to bed-wetting involves reinforcing dryness at night. The specifics of handling bed-wetting, however, are a bit different from daytime strategies.

Bed-wetting is the kind of difficulty that becomes defined as a problem by virtue of a child's age. No one, for example, is concerned because a one-year-old wets the bed because no one-year-old child has yet mastered the self-control needed to avoid wetting at nighttime (and at other times). But when the same child is four or five years old and still has this self-control problem, most parents become concerned, and appropriately so. In general, about one year after a child has become consistently toilet trained during the day, the parent can consider frequent bed-wetting at night a problem. It is desirable to help your child overcome bed-wetting just as soon as it becomes evident that this is a problem. Otherwise the child is likely over time to experience embarrassment, shame, and feelings of inadequacy because of the continuing bed-wetting difficulty. The longer a bed-wetting pattern has gone on, the more likely it will be that the child will come to believe that he *cannot* control it, making change even more difficult.

If your child wets the bed, we first recommend a visit to your family doctor or pediatrician. Just as daytime accidents can have medical causes, bed-wetting can be the result of a physical malfunction that reduces the child's degree of bladder control. Certain diseases, urinary infections, and sleep pattern problems can contribute to bed-wetting, and your physician can determine whether these are responsible. In the majority of cases such physically based factors are not present, but it is important to have your child checked by a doctor.

It is useful to view bed-wetting as a problem in which the child currently lacks a self-control skill. Consequently, the most effective way to solve this problem is by reinforcing the child's attempts to stay dry at night. Rather than punishing the child who wets the bed (thereby creating destructive guilt and embarrassment), we want to strengthen the child's own capacity to control bed-wetting. Before you begin to work on this problem with your child, it is most useful to keep track of exactly how often your child wets the bed over a one- to two-week period. We suggest that you keep these records — even if the wetting occurs every night — so that you will later be able to measure your progress. Most parents find it hard to recall, for example, how many times their child wet the bed three weeks ago. Without that kind of accurate information on hand it will be difficult for you to tell whether the child is doing better now than he was a short time ago. For a one- or two-week period, list the days of the week and note whether the child wet the bed each night.

After this record-keeping period you are ready to begin solving the problem with your child. We advocate a two-level set of procedures to control bed-wetting. The first procedure is the easiest to implement for both child and parent, and has been effective in a large number of our clinic cases, especially if the child has had at least some nights in his or her life when no bed-wetting occurred. If this technique is not successful we advise the parent to move on to the second-level procedure. Let's look at them.

BED-WETTING SELF-CONTROL: THE FIRST STEP

The initial way to handle bed-wetting involves several tasks: reducing the child's need to urinate after going to sleep, strongly rewarding the child for having had a dry night, and arranging for the child to take clean-up responsibilities for mornings after bed-wetting has occurred. These steps are started simultaneously because overcoming bed-wetting usually requires the combined effect of all of them. Begin by establishing a cutoff time for evening liquids. A good rule is for the child to have no liquids within two full hours of bedtime. We also ask the parent to have the child use the bathroom twice before bedtime; the first use should be about thirty minutes before bed and the second immediately before bed. The child should do this each night, even if he doesn't feel a strong need to use the bathroom. If the child does urinate on these occasions before bed, praise him for doing so.

Because we want to increase the child's self-control behavior, it is important that we develop a plan for strongly rewarding dry nights. This can be done with a dry-night chart such as the one shown in figure 3. The chart lists the days of the week, and beneath each day provides a box in which you can place a star if the child is dry on that night. Several weeks can be illustrated on one chart, which should be taped in a conspicuous place on a wall or door in the child's bedroom. We see in the figure that Johnny had three dry nights in the first week, in the second and third weeks five dry nights, and six nights in the final period.

When your child is on this system, you should do the following:

In the morning, immediately after the child wakes up, check

FIGURE 3

Johnny's A Big Boy Now!

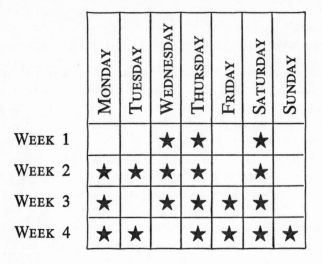

	MONDAY	TUESDAY	WEDNESDAY	THURSDAY	FRIDAY	SATURDAY	SUNDAY
WEEK 1			★	★		★	
WEEK 2	★	★	★	★		★	
WEEK 3	★		★	★	★	★	
WEEK 4	★	★		★	★	★	★

the bed for wetness. If the bed is wet, do not scold or criticize the child. Remember that we don't want to punish the child's failure but to strongly reinforce his successes. If a wet night occurs, explain to your child in a matter-of-fact way that you're sorry he had a wetting episode, he won't be able to get the special rewards today for being dry, but that tonight will be a new night and he can try again. The tone of this explanation should be firm but constructive and encouraging. Nonetheless, if the child does have a wet night, he or she should be required to assume some responsibility for clean-up of the bed. Although mildly unpleasant, it is better for the child to have this responsibility than for you to do it. Have the child remove the soiled sheets and other linen, place them in the clothes hamper or washing machine and, if the child is old enough, start the wash. This should be done first thing in the morning, right after you have checked the bed and found it wet.

If the child has a dry bed when you check it in the morning, strongly reward his success. This is critical: a dry night should be viewed as a highly commendable accomplishment (which it *is* to a child who has had a bed-wetting problem), and the parent should lavishly praise the child's success at staying dry that night. Tell your child that you feel proud of him, that the child did well, and that he is becoming a grown-up now. As you are giving this praise, mark a big star on the chart. Better still, let the child proudly mark his or her own star.

While verbal praise is necessary, it is not enough. Back it up with a more concrete reward. Before beginning the dry-night program, we suggest that you and your child arrange some event that the child enjoys to follow a dry night. In our clinic children who had bed-wetting problems have been rewarded with trips to McDonald's or an ice cream store the afternoon following a dry night, with a special twenty-minute time to spend playing catch with Dad on the morning the child was dry, and with special spending allowances given first thing in the morning after a dry night. As for other types of reward-based programs, whichever tangible reinforcer you use must be something that is rewarding and special in your child's eyes and something that can be provided every day when the child has been dry the preceding night. Have your child help you pick what those special rewards will be before the program is started. Plan to follow this program consistently every day. Because it involves reinforcing your child's self-control efforts, it is important that your child learn to anticipate that all kinds of good things will happen on mornings when the bed is dry. Don't ever take dry nights for granted until bed-wetting has long since been overcome and the child is routinely able to control the problem.

We have found that this program tends to improve children's bed-wetting quite gradually, rather than immediately. That is one reason why we ask parents to keep track of wet nights/dry nights for up to two weeks before starting the program and to record how many dry nights are achieved each week that the system is in effect thereafter. At the end of each week, compare the number of dry nights with those of past weeks. So long as general improvement is evident, and even if there are occasional relapses, keep up the same program. If it appears at any point that your child has become bored with the concrete rewards you are using, develop new ones that will rekindle your child's motivation.

If the program has been in effect for some time (usually four to six weeks) and no improvement is evident, a still stronger system will be needed.

THE SECOND STEP TO CONTROL BED-WETTING

This more intensified program starts off with all the same elements we've just described: No liquids for two hours before bed, using the bathroom one half hour and then immediately before bedtime, lavish praise and tangible rewards for each dry night, and the child's responsibility for sheet-changing following wet nights. However if those steps alone are sufficient, we then must make it easier for the child to be able to have a night without wetting and thus to begin succeeding. At this point, build into the system the following additional procedures:

Nighttime wake-ups to use the bathroom. By waking your child during the night so that he or she can quickly use the bathroom and then go back to sleep, you will be reducing the likelihood of an accident. The most convenient time to do this is usually right before you go to bed. He may not like this, but get your child up anyway, even if he reports no need to use the toilet. If the child does actually use it, offer praise and remind the child that it is good to get up to use the bathroom if he should wake up and feel the need to do so.

The bed-wet alarm. A commercial device can actually alert your child when he or she begins to bed-wet. The most widely available device of this kind is called the Wee Alert

Alarm and is sold nationally by Sears and Roebuck in its stores and catalogue. This modestly priced unit consists of a pad that fits under the sheet. The first hint of moisture touching the pad completes a small electrical circuit that causes an alarm to sound. The alarm is loud enough to immediately awaken the child so that he can use the bathroom before a serious wetting episode has occurred. This device is most useful for children over five, since very young children can be startled by the alarm and not remember why it is sounding. Operated by a small battery, the device is safe and effective.

We recommend that parents consider using such an alarm if the previously outlined steps alone have been unsuccessful in reducing the child's bed-wetting problem. If an alarm device is used, however, it should always be in the context of a total program that includes all the earlier steps. A bed-wet alarm alerts the child to get up and use the bathroom only after a wetting episode has already started; it's the moisture that activates the alarm. Although this may be necessary for difficult bed-wetters, the parent also needs to be reinforcing the child's self-control so the alarm can gradually be discontinued. The best way to do this is by using the kind of reward-based system we outlined earlier, even when the alarm is also used.

The first-step technique and, if it needs to be added, the second-step technique enable many children to overcome bed-wetting problems, usually within one to two months. They must, of course, be diligently followed by the parent until wetting has been completely eliminated. In a relatively small number of instances, bed-wetting may be resistant even to these procedures; outside help should then be considered (see chapter 10). Behavioral psychologists have developed specialized procedures that teach children how to control bladder tension (in essence helping them to hold off the need to urinate for longer periods). This training, although not necessary for most children, does require that the parent obtain the advice of a professional.

HOW TO HANDLE CURIOSITY ABOUT
SEX AND SEX PLAY

Probably more than any other aspect of human behavior, matters involving sex seem able to create anxiety, uncertainty, and, in general, to bring out the worst fears in otherwise rational adults. And when the subject is evidence of the sexual curiosity of their own children, it is not surprising that many parents are a bit unsure about how they should react. Although parents expect that sex is an issue they will face (often with some combination of trepidation and dread) when their children become adolescents, they seem even more concerned and confused about handling the sexual curiosity of their young children.

Reactions to children's sexual behavior tend to run to extremes. For most of the years since the Victorian era, society in general (and parents in particular) seemed to believe that children shouldn't show any interest or curiosity about sex. If they did, that curiosity was quickly stifled and the child was made to feel that even having such interest was wrong. In contrast to this enduring and repressive attitude, parents in the 1950s began to hear just the opposite message: children's curiosity about sex should be encouraged and promoted in any way possible. According to this view, if a parent does anything at all to inhibit the child's sexual exploration, the youngster's natural feelings will be constrained and an anxious neuroticism about sex will be fostered.

As is so often the case, a sound course for parents undoubtedly lies somewhere between these extremes. We know now that children do have a natural and innocent curiosity about sex, and we have reason to believe that if parents become threatened and emotionally defensive when they find evidence of this interest, their children may develop anxieties related to sexuality. But as we will see, it is possible for parents to handle a child's sexual curiosity in a way that is truthful and provides both acceptance and guidance to the youngster.

In this way, the appropriate and positive handling of a child's natural curiosity about sex can prevent the issue from later becoming a behavior or self-control problem.

Why are children curious about sex? Youngsters are curious about their whole bodies. We adults take our bodies pretty much for granted, but children are still fascinated even by the fact that they have hands, arms, legs, feet . . . and genitals. Coupled with this fascination, children learn that certain parts of their bodies result in pleasure, such as their mouths for eating and their noses for smelling pleasant things. They find that their genitals can likewise be a source of pleasurable feelings.

One mistake parents sometimes make lies in equating a child's early, natural inquisitiveness about sex with the kind of mature sexual behavior and feelings experienced by adults. The two are very different. In contrast to adults, the curiosity of young children is part of a more general interest in their entire bodies. If a child asks his parent what an ear is for, the parent calmly explains it. But if the child then asks what a penis is for, the parent becomes nervous and upset. To a young child this difference in reactions is puzzling because the questions are really quite similar and they are being asked for the same reason: The youngster is simply curious. A second difference between adult and child sexuality involves the nature of pleasurable feelings themselves. While adults have feelings that can be specifically labeled as sexual, the feelings of young children are simply sensual or pleasurable in a much more general way. Self-fondling or self-touching means something different to a young child than it does to an adult.

How should parents react to a child's self-fondling? Occasional self-touching and masturbation are universal and normal among children and do not represent problems that need your attention at all. As youngsters reach school age, they tend to be less preoccupied with their bodies and self-play usually decreases by itself. A few children, however, develop the habit of spending long periods of time continually holding their genitals. This, by the way, is much more a habit than an indication of anything sexual. If it happens, explain to your youngster that you don't want him to have this habit and, when you notice what you think will be a period of extended self-touching, direct and guide the child's hands to some other activity. Then, offer praise and let the youngster know that, especially when he is in a public place, it is better to do things with hands rather than holding onto oneself. This sort of matter-of-fact redirection is usually all that is needed, although you may need to repeat it from time to time.

How should parents react to a child's sex play with other children? If children are curious about their own bodies, they can be almost as curious about the bodies of others. For this reason it is also quite common for children, especially four- to six-year-olds, to show interest in one another's anatomy. Such play is not an indication that there is anything wrong with the youngster; it can best be viewed as a generally short phase in a child's development. On the other hand, it is reasonable for parents to make their children aware that engaging in sex play with others is not appropriate. If you observe such an episode, you should direct the youngster to stop. However, do this in a calm and matter-of-fact way, without emotional overreaction. If your child is over four, have a short talk about the subject of playing with others in a sexual way. In the discussion, explain that you understand the child was only playing, but also let the youngster know that this is not the way you want him to play with others. You might want to discuss the idea of privacy, explaining that some parts of the body are his own and are not for play with other people. Finally, end your short talk by giving the child a few examples of appropriate play activities and convey that you want him to do these things instead with his friends. When you next see your own child and the other youngster playing appropriately, be sure to praise the child for this better conduct.

What should I say when my child asks me questions about

sex? Parents are sometimes uncertain how to answer their children's questions about sex. Actually, young children very rarely ask questions that deal with sexual behavior as most adults think of the term. Kids are much more likely to ask simple questions about parts of their body ("Mommy, what is this?") or about the nature of life ("Where did I come from?" or "How is my new little brother or sister going to get here?").

These are all very genuine and very reasonable questions for children to ask and they need not cause you embarrassment. Questions of this kind call for honest answers. All that is really required is for you to respond in a manner that is accurate and is presented at a level your youngster is able to understand. Don't feel the need to overexplain. Especially when they know you will not be upset or embarrassed, children tend to ask questions at their own rates and at the times and levels of sophistication they require. So when a four-year-old asks his mother where he came from, the parent might simply explain that she and his father were in love and decided they wanted to have a child. Or when a child of the same age asks what his genitals are for, the parent could explain that they are something that boys are born with. As your youngster gets older and asks more specific questions, he or she will probably be ready for correspondingly more detailed answers.

HOW TO HANDLE DAWDLING

Dawdling can be a real problem for families whose five- and six-year-old children do it. Dawdling means that the child takes an exceptionally long time to do something, most commonly in the morning or at bedtime. Morning dawdlers manage to get ready for school but only in the nick of time, and only after a good deal of reminding and progressively more frantic yelling on the part of the parent ("C'mon, it's twenty minutes to eight and you're not even dressed yet," "Hurry *up!*" "If you don't get ready this minute you'll be walking to school because you'll miss the bus," and so on). This can be a major problem in families where everyone is heading off to work or school at the same time in the morning, including parents who don't always have the time to tolerate excessive dawdling. In one case treated in our clinic, the parent had been so unable to control the child's dawdling that she found herself spanking her son every morning. It's not an ideal way to start the day, for the parent or the child. Dawdling at night usually takes place when the child wants to put off getting ready for bed by avoiding brushing teeth, taking a bath, and so on. These tasks may eventually happen, but only after a great deal of parental nagging.

The way many parents handle dawdling proves that nagging or threatening punishment often fails to work. We advocate a system that rewards the child for getting ready more promptly. One of the best procedures to use is a game called Beat the Buzzer, developed by Dr. Ronald Drabman at the University of Mississippi Medical Center. Easy and effective to use, children almost invariably find the technique fun. Here's how it works.

First, decide what time you want your child to be ready for something. If the child must be ready to leave the house for school in the morning by 8:00, you'll probably want him to be all ready to go by 7:50. Next, decide how long it should take your child to get dressed, cleaned up, and set to leave. Let's say this is twenty minutes, although the actual time will depend on the things your child has to do in the morning. That means the child could be ready to leave at 7:50 if he or she started at 7:30 and got dressed and cleaned up without dawdling.

To use Beat the Buzzer in this case, the parent takes a kitchen timer and at 7:30 sets it to ring in twenty minutes. (If you don't have a timer you can buy one for a few dollars at most hardware or department stores.) It will be the child's job to be ready before the timer's bell rings. For every minute the child beats the buzz by, he or she can stay up an extra ten minutes past the usual bedime later that evening. For every minute the child takes to get ready after the timer rings, the child must go to bed ten minutes earlier than usual that night. The aim of the child, of course, quickly becomes beating the buzzer by as many minutes as possible. Thus, the system reinforces the desired behavior (promptness) and carries with it a mild loss of privileges (earlier to bed) in the unlikely event the child continues to dawdle.

This simple procedure works well for almost all dawdlers. If your child dawdles in the evening (rather than in the morning), it can be used in the same manner. A parent should keep several things in mind when setting up Beat the Buzzer, however. The period you set on the timer should be such that the child can beat it by at least a few minutes when he doesn't dawdle. If the best he can do is be ready when it rings, the child will never actually be rewarded for promptness because he won't be earning any later-to-bed time. The system cannot work under these circumstances. On the other hand, if the timer is set for too long and your child can beat it with ages to spare, you may find your youngster still awake at midnight enjoying his success!

Be sure to decide with your child exactly what being ready means. Often it's good to explicitly list the required tasks ("brush teeth," "wash face and hands," "have school clothes on") to avoid a situation in which the child says "I'm ready" but the parent feels he hasn't really done everything. Finally, staying up a bit later than usual is something most children find pleasurable, but other kinds of reinforcers can just as easily be substituted in this program.

7/
Helping Your Child Overcome Fears

IMAGINE finding yourself one day in a place that is unfamiliar and strange to you, where you don't know many people. Imagine further that something unpleasant or frightening has recently happened to you in this new place, or that you have just seen something bad happen to another person you know. Under these circumstances, our natural reaction is to feel fear. Whenever we are in a place that is unknown, or when we are exposed to a situation in which something distressing has already occurred, our immediate reaction is to experience fright. Only after we've grown comfortable in the situation and learned over time that nothing bad is going to happen do we become at ease. Very few people grow up without some fears that must be overcome, and even well-adjusted children who have warm, reassuring parents may develop isolated fears. While the range of things that can frighten children is almost endless, the most common childhood fears seen in our clinic include fears of the dark and of sleeping alone (which are especially likely to be problems for three- and four-year-olds), fear of animals, and fear of doctors and hospitals (which are often problems for older children). As we will see, these as well as most other childhood fears can be solved using the same general approach.

Before we turn our attention to the matter of solving the problem of children's unreasonable fears, let's consider why children develop fears in the first place and then look at some of the misguided strategies parents occasionally use to try to overcome them.

WHY IS MY CHILD AFRAID?

Children's fears tend to develop from three kinds of causes: (1) something bad actually happened to the child in a situation similar to the one now feared, (2) the child has seen or heard about something bad happening to someone else in that situation, or (3) a situation is so unfamiliar or different that it leads to a generalized fear of the unknown.

FEARS STEMMING FROM DIRECT EXPERIENCE

The most direct and understandable fears are those that develop because a child has actually had something bad, frightening, or embarrassing happen to him in a situation similar to the present one. In essence it is a trauma-caused fear. The youngster who was once bitten by a dog and now is afraid of dogs (and perhaps even other animals) is a classic example. A child who became lost in a large department store can develop a fear of being away from his parents; the youngster who accidentally tumbled into the deep end of a swimming pool may later become terrified of water.

Experiences don't have to be dramatically traumatic to cause fears. Many children become fearful of trips to the doctor or the dentist not because the doctor has intentionally terrorized them but because the youngster has learned that painful things often take place there. Similarly, the child who has few athletic skills can become fearful of competitive baseball games if that situation in the past repeatedly led to embarrassment or failure.

FEARS BASED ON THE EXPERIENCES OF OTHERS

In chapter 4 we saw how modeling (or learning by watching others) influences children's behavior. Kids can acquire fears by observing the unpleasant experiences of others or, even more indirectly, by being told about dangerous things that might happen to them. This sort of learning often accounts for the development of fears that parents cannot explain, because the triggering incidents may occur beyond parental supervision. Seeing a violent and frightening horror movie isn't likely to traumatize most adults because we have learned to tell ourselves that this is only entertainment. The same movie seen by a young child, who has less ability to reassure himself that it is only make-believe, can produce long-lasting fearfulness. Occasionally parents inadvertently create fears by telling their children that some terrible (and untrue) thing will happen if they misbehave. Being told that you can lose your genitals for masturbating or that you can give your mother a heart attack when she has to work hard to pick up your toys may temporarily improve the conduct of a young child but it can also foster extraordinary guilt and fear in the process, especially when the five- or six-year-old child accepts these statements as fact.

In our clinic we once saw a young child preoccupied by dying and not going to heaven. Upon questioning the parents we learned that the child had occasionally been told, "God won't take you to heaven if you talk back to your parents." Unintentionally, these parents were encouraging the development of a very difficult and guilt-related fear in their child. Clearly, one should never attempt to manipulate a child's behavior using threats that are untrue and can only induce fear.

If we view nightmares as a form of modeling — in which a person's behavior is affected by something he sees in dreams — the content of nightmares can also create or aggravate fears. While many nightmare frights pass quickly when the youngster awakens, recurrent dreams about topics that are already frightening to the child (say, dreaming about a vicious dog after a child has been bitten) can serve to strengthen the youngster's actual fear.

FEAR OF NEW SITUATIONS

A third kind of fear can develop as a child is exposed to new situations for the first time, even when nothing bad has directly happened to cause this feeling or fright. Fear of leaving home and going to nursery school or elementary school are good examples, as is the fear of meeting strangers for the first time. The sheer novelty of being placed in a new situation, especially one in which familiar sources of support (such as a parent's presence) are missing, creates anxiety for some children.

Interestingly, studies have shown that even newborn infants vary in their reactions to novel and unfamiliar stimuli. Some infants seem to seek out and truly enjoy being in unfamiliar settings, being held by different people, and exploring uncharted environments. Other infants have a low tolerance for the unknown and the unfamiliar, becoming easily upset even by slight changes in their everyday routines. There seem to be constitutional (and perhaps genetic) differences in the responses of infants to new situations, with extreme fearfulness on one end of the spectrum and extreme fearlessness on the other. Just where on this range of reactions a particular infant is located may increase that youngster's later tendency to be fearful in new situations.

Up to this point we have tended to focus on children's fears as being undesirable. This is true, of course, when a child experiences unpleasant emotional reactions in situations that are really harmless. But before we all start wishing we had fearless, John Wayne-style youngsters, consider how difficult it would really be to raise such a child. He or she would forever be running amok in the streets and into the paths of oncoming cars, pulling hot skillets off stovetops, diving headfirst into the deep ends of swimming pools, jumping down stairs with open scissors in hand, and wandering off with strangers on every trip to the shopping mall. Given that all children do some of these things once in a while, imagine how hard it would be to contend with nonstop fearlessness. A bit of fear is not only a human but also an adaptive quality which literally permits kids to survive their own childhoods. It's only at the point when children become overly frightened of harmless things that parents should intervene to allay the child's fears.

SOME COMMON (BUT INCORRECT) APPROACHES FOR REDUCING CHILDREN'S FEARS

There are three relatively common methods parents use to try to help their children overcome fears. Each approach works some of the time, but each also carries the potential for creating still other difficulties. Let's briefly look at them.

1. AFRAID OF WATER? THEN SINK OR SWIM

The sink-or-swim strategy is based on the notion that the best way for a child to overcome fears is to face them head-on, cold turkey, and with no chance for escape. The child who is afraid of water gets tossed into a swimming pool, the youngster afraid of dogs is locked in a house with one, the child afraid of being hurt is dragged to a football game and made to play quarterback. The idea is that once you've gone through the feared situation and survived it, your fear will disappear, an idea not altogether incorrect. Forced exposure to what one fears is actually the basis for a clinical technique sometimes used to treat irrational fears (or phobias) that adults experience. But serious problems and potentially undesirable side-effects may arise when parents impose this solution on their children. One problem is that this technique may actually intensify conflict and terror for the young child who finds himself facing something fearful and lacks any way to cope with the anxiety. If the youngster's fear is very great and if sudden forced exposure doesn't entirely eliminate it the first time, the child will be even more terrified in the future. Even more important, making a child do something he fears in one sudden step can seriously jeopardize the child's faith and trust in his parent.

2. GIVING IN TO YOUR CHILD'S FEARS

This strategy is exactly the opposite of sink-or-swim. In the giving-in approach, the parent allows the child to completely avoid whatever he or she fears. For example, the first response of a child who is afraid of being alone in the dark is usually to go to his parents' room and try to sleep there. With very young children this is not an overwhelming problem for a parent to tolerate occasionally. But it often establishes a precedent for the child to sleep with his parents, thereby avoiding the task of overcoming the fear. Routinely sleeping with parents can undermine the child's development of self-reliance and can impinge on the parents' own right to have time alone together. Whenever parents give in to their youngster's fears they prevent the child from having the opportunity to master whatever he is afraid of. While keeping children away from frightening situations is a convenient and easy thing to do, it only postpones and complicates dealing with the problem. It does not solve it.

3. TELLING A LIE

Some children's fears can actually turn honest parents into liars! Probably the classic, most common example of this occurs when a child is about to go to the pediatrician for a shot and is reassured that it won't hurt when the parent knows that shots do hurt. The strategy of telling a child something that's not true to lessen the youngster's fears is almost always well-intentioned and does work — but only the first time. Afterward the child will know, first that his fear was warranted, and second that you can't even believe your own parents in such matters.

Rather than trying to reduce a child's fears by being dishonest (if well meaning), it is far better to tell the child what will really happen but in a reassuring and positive tone. A child who is fearful because he is about to enter the hospital for an operation should not be told that nothing will hurt or that the experience will be fun if it isn't going to be. It is far better to briefly but accurately explain what will happen, that some things may hurt a little bit, but that this happens to many people and the child will get through it fine. If possible you might draw upon similar experiences you have had and tell how you successfully managed them. This is a far more effective strategy for lessening a child's fear than providing empty reassurances that you know are untrue.

PROGRESSIVE EXPOSURE: AN EFFECTIVE FEAR-REDUCTION PLAN

Progressive Exposure is an effective, structured, and planned approach to fear reduction that can reduce your child's anxiety and increase his self-confidence. The rationale for Progressive Exposure is straightforward. If you are afraid of something that can't really harm you, the best way to get over it is by being placed in a warm, positive environment and being systematically and increasingly exposed to what you are afraid of. As you find that nothing bad will happen and as you gain confidence in your ability to handle what once was feared, your anxiety will disappear. This approach is different from forced, sudden exposure because it takes place in graded, successive, and positive steps. And it's different from simply avoiding what one fears because the child is always required to take those steps. Not only are parents pleased to see their children overcome fears, but youngsters are usually just as eager to feel unafraid.

Let's see how the Progressive Exposure approach can be applied to one very common childhood problem, fear of the dark. We'll then discuss its application to other kinds of fears.

OVERCOMING FEAR OF THE DARK

Drs. Stan O'Dell and Jean Giebenhain, child psychologists at the University of Mississippi, have developed a program for treating children who are afraid of the dark. Usually this fear becomes evident when a youngster is unable to go to sleep in his or her own room at night with the lights off. Sometimes these children can go to sleep in the security of their parents' room, while at other times they will fall asleep only in a brightly lit room.

To solve this problem, a parent's first task is to plan a series of progressive, graded steps that fall between what the child can now do without fear and the final goal. Arranging these steps is a critical part of the fear-solving process: we want the first step to be what your child can already do and we want each successive step to be only slightly more difficult for your child to attain, always moving in the direction of the final goal. If the distance between one step and the next more difficult step is too great, your child won't be able to master it successfully. In the fear of the dark example, the steps involve being able to go to sleep alone in slowly decreasing amounts of room light.

If your child is afraid of the dark, begin things with a trip to the local hardware store to buy a rheostat dimmer switch for a couple of dollars. The dimmer switch replaces the standard on-off light switch in your child's room; its dial gradually changes the brightness of the light in degrees. When the dimmer device is attached to the light switch on your child's bedroom wall, use a crayon to mark about eight points on the dial, with the first mark at the totally bright position and the last mark at totally dark. The other marks are placed at equal distances between the two extremes. Each mark indicates a barely noticeable reduction in brightness compared to the one before it. Based on how frightened your child is of the dark, pick the mark that represents the amount of light your child now prefers for sleeping. This will be the first step of our Progressive Exposure program.

On the night you want to start solving this problem, explain to your child that you have developed a game that will help him get over his fear of the dark. Explain that the game will be fun rather than scary, and that by the end of the game he won't be afraid of the dark anymore, just as older kids aren't. The game rules are these:

1. Beginning on the first night, your child will sleep in his room with the light set at the intensity with which he now feels comfortable; if this means sleeping in a completely bright room, that is acceptable. Start off at whatever mark on the dimmer device your child prefers.

2. Once bedtime arrives, your child must stay in his room all night, again with the light intensity kept at the mark you and your youngster selected.

3. At bedtime, reassure your child that you know he'll do fine tonight and that he will get a special treat or activity in the morning for sleeping in his own room all night. Make a success chart like the one in figure 4 and tape it to the door of the child's bedroom.

4. In the event your child does leave his room (other than for a necessary trip to the bathroom), immediately take the child back. Tell him that if he leaves again, he will lose the special reward in the morning. Beyond this point, the reward incentive for the morning is lost, but continue to return the child to his room whenever it is necessary. It is important that he learn that he will spend the night there, even if it means several return trips during the night.

5. In the morning, we want to strongly reinforce the child for having slept in his room with the light set at the selected mark. Do this in several ways. First, praise the child for staying in the bedroom with the light at its set level. Be generous in your praise and really help your child feel proud of this accomplishment. As you do this,

FIGURE 4

Tommy's Getting Over His Fear of the Dark!

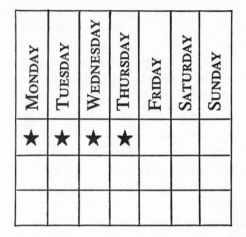

MONDAY	TUESDAY	WEDNESDAY	THURSDAY	FRIDAY	SATURDAY	SUNDAY
★	★	★	★			

help the child make a big star on the success chart for that night's achievement. Back up your praise with a special and tangible reward of the kind described in chapter 2. Never forget to reinforce a successful night, and always do it with enthusiasm! A good place for this announcement is at the breakfast table, where everyone in the family can congratulate the child.

6. Follow the same procedure each night until your child has been successful at the first dial setting for three nights in a row. Then you're ready to move to the next mark, to make the room a bit darker, but just barely so. Again, after three successful nights in a row have been achieved at this slightly darker light level, the dimmer switch is moved to its next lower mark for the following evening.

7. As the program moves along, your child will gradually be adapting to an ever-darkening room. Even as you get to the last marks (and an almost dark room), keep handling successful nights in the same way and keep re-

turning the child to his room should he leave it. Never go backward on the dial to increase the light setting from the previous night; the light either stays the same or is reduced. Finally, as the light intensity reaches the lowest setting, put a small night light into one of the room's electrical outlets and leave the main room light completely off. At this point your child's fear of the dark will be solved! Congratulate his accomplishment and over the next few weeks periodically let the youngster know you are proud of his success.

As you can see, the elements of this Progressive Exposure approach are fairly straightforward. Once we decide on a final goal (in this case, sleeping with the lights off), we can arrange small steps that will gradually but progressively expose the child to what he fears. Because that exposure is gradual, success-oriented, and because the parent strongly reinforces each step of the child's improvement, mastery is fun rather than threatening to the child. With this positive approach, most children are able to overcome their fear of the dark in several weeks.

OVERCOMING THE FEAR OF SLEEPING ALONE

A related and common fear among children involves sleeping alone. Occasionally this accompanies being afraid of the dark, while at other times the fear is specific to the idea of being alone in the bedroom all night. Fear of sleeping alone is fairly widespread among children under four and occasionally persists well beyond this age, especially for children used to sleeping with someone else. As long as this fear persists it is difficult for a youngster to feel independent and self-sufficient.

The basic strategy for overcoming this fear is quite similar to the approach we described for getting over fear of the dark. We will need to establish a series of steps between your child's current level of fear and the final goal of sleeping alone in his own room. Instead of steps that involve progressively lower amounts of light in a room, we will want to create steps that involve decreasing physical proximity to the parents at night to allow the child to gradually adjust to the habit of sleeping alone.

First Step. This is the status quo: whatever goes on right now. For most children who are afraid to sleep by themselves it means staying in the parents' room and probably in the parents' bed.

Second Step: At this point our only aim is to get the child out of the parents' bed. If a child is intensely afraid of sleeping by himself, it may be too great a step to require him to sleep in his own room immediately. So for this intermediate phase, if necessary, the child can sleep on a mattress placed temporarily on the floor in his parents' room. The child will sleep in a bed by himself but will still have his or her parents nearby at night. Remember, though, that once he's at this stage the youngster should never be permitted back in his parents' bed. If this happens, immediately return your child to his own sleeping place and ask that he stay there.

Third Step: Now we're ready for the child to move to his own bed and his own room, but with the parent present to provide security. At bedtime your child will go to his own room, but one parent (it doesn't matter which) will stay with him until he falls asleep. This is probably the toughest stage for the parent, entailing as it does a good deal of time in the child's room. This is a good opportunity to pull out the bedtime storybook, read a pleasant story to your child, and then turn down the lights and wait until he falls asleep. Then, quietly leave. If your child later wakes up and comes to your room, he must immediately be taken back to his own bed and asked to remain there. Don't sit up with him again at this point. Whenever your child back-slides and tries to sleep with you, immediately follow this procedure, even if it means several trips a night. Once your child learns that you will be firm on this point, the problem will virtually be solved.

Fourth Step: After your youngster has adapted to the habit of sleeping in his room all night, your only remaining task is to help him fall asleep without your physical presence. When you've reached this point, go into your child's room as he climbs into bed and sit down near him. Read the child a nighttime story, especially if you've been doing this in the preceding step, and let him say his prayers if he does so at night. Then reassure your child that you will be nearby all night but that he or she can sleep alone now just like big children do. Quietly leave the room.

Parents can teach their children to sleep alone by following this progression of steps that gradually move closer to the final objective. We again suggest that you allow the child to do well at each level for at least three consecutive nights before you move on to the next step, and never move backward in the program, even for a single night. Remember also that how you handle your child's nightly successes is always critical. Introduce the plan to your youngster as a positive game in which he or she will learn to act grown-up and will be able to sleep alone. Be lavish in your praise every morning the child has done well; as your child sees that you are visibly proud of his accomplishment the night before, he will try harder to be independent and will feel more confident. Put a success chart (like that shown in figure 4) on the child's bedroom wall and help the child mark a big star (accompanied by your praise, of course) every morning after a success. Finally, be sure to include a special reward or activity you know your child enjoys the morning after every successful night. Even if you had to return the child to his own room several times during the night, praise the child but tell him you will be happier yet when he stays there all by himself.

OVERCOMING THE FEAR OF ANIMALS

Pets may provide some of the fondest recollections from our childhoods. Most kids love animals, and being around pets provides an opportunity for children to learn the importance of respecting life. It also allows them to direct their early-life concern and comparison to objects outside themselves. While it isn't reasonable to expect a young child to provide sole care for an animal, as kids start to get older they can take on at least some of the responsibilities for their pet's care. Even at that unhappy time when an old, loved pet dies, children can gain what is really the very positive and important opportunity to experience grief and thereby learn about the nature of life and death. This is the sort of experience that can actually prepare a child to handle death and losses later in his or her life.

However, the classic happy-boy-and-his-dog (or girl and her dog) story doesn't always happen in quite this way. Some youngsters are literally terrified of animals. In the most extreme case a child may be so frightened of dogs that he won't leave the house or walk down the street if an animal is anywhere nearby. Sometimes this fear stems from an unpleasant real-life encounter (such as being bitten or otherwise frightened by an animal). At other times the origin of the fear is more difficult to pinpoint. Earlier in the chapter we noted that fear is not always a bad human characteristic: it can serve a useful purpose by keeping us away from situations that really are dangerous. Some animals can be vicious and some dogs do bite. For their own safety, children should never be encouraged to approach unfamiliar animals; keeping a certain degree of wariness is wise and parents shouldn't try to eliminate it. Most adults can tell a friendly from an unfriendly dog by noticing subtleties in the way the animal reacts when it is approached. But young children can't yet make this distinction, and the wise parent will warn his or her youngster against approaching unfamiliar animals.

What, though, can a parent do when a child is unreasonably terrified of a pet that is known to be friendly, or when a child has such an unrealistic fear of animals that he is frightened to leave his home or yard? Again, the strategy of Progressive Exposure is used to overcome this fear. Let's look at one case that illustrates how this approach can lessen a terror of dogs.

Six-year-old Cindy was brought to our clinic by her mother because the parent was concerned about her daughter's increasing terror of dogs. Cindy's mother told us that her daughter had gone to a neighbor's house about a year ago and walked into the neighbor's back yard, where a small dog was kept. The little but ill-tempered animal began barking at Cindy and actually nipped her on the leg, badly frightening her. After this incident the parent properly cautioned her daughter not to approach this dog or other strange animals. Unfortunately, the child's fear of dogs increased and she developed nightmares about dogs chasing her, became terrified of going outside until someone checked to see whether any dogs were around, and was even afraid to visit her aunt's home because the woman had a large dog.

In Cindy's case fear had grown from a normal and healthy fear of a specific dog to an unrealistic fear of all animals that actually curtailed her activities. To help Cindy get over this fear, we developed a plan to progressively expose her to the object of her fright. As in overcoming fear of the dark or fear of sleeping alone, our plan again involved creating steps; in this case the steps would be designed to bring her gradually closer to friendly dogs.

Because Cindy's aunt lived near her, and because the aunt's dog was known to be friendly, our Progressive Exposure practice took place with that dog. If the aunt had not been there, we would have located some other friendly dog. The first step of our plan was for Cindy and her mother to visit the aunt's house one afternoon. The dog was to remain securely tied outside in the back yard the entire time that Cindy, her mother, and her aunt all stayed inside. This was chosen as a first step in the plan because, although not very enthusiastic about it, Cindy did agree to go there as a result of reassurance that the dog couldn't get into the house. If Cindy had been too frightened even for that starting point, we would have begun with a still easier first step (such as sitting in her mother's car in front of the aunt's house). Progressive Exposure always begins with something the child *can* do. Cindy's mother was told to bring favorite games to the aunt's house so her daughter would have a pleasant time playing there and would almost forget to worry about the dog. At the end of a half-hour visit, the mother warmly praised Cindy for having stayed at her aunt's home even though the feared pet was nearby. These visits were repeated several times over a one-week period until the child had entirely overcome her fear of this early step.

The next phase of the plan had Cindy visit her aunt's house again, but now she was asked occasionally to look out the back window at the dog, which was still kept outside during her visits. As she looked at the pet, mother told her child reassuring things like "Red is a nice dog. He likes people," or "That dog would like you, I bet." If Cindy replied that she was frightened or showed any signs of fear, the parent was instructed to calmly remind Cindy that she need not be afraid of Red because "he's a nice dog." This step — simply watching the dog while being given gentle reassurances by her mother — was also repeated until Cindy could watch the dog through the window without fear.

Our third step made use of modeling. Cindy remained in the house but watched as her mother went outside to pet Red. Here, the mother was a model for the daughter to observe. Cindy's fears diminished as she watched her mother petting the dog and saw that she was not being hurt. Mom later told Cindy how much she had enjoyed petting Red, further making clear that petting the dog could be a positive experience.

Additional steps moved Cindy closer to the final goal. When Cindy had grown accustomed to seeing her mother pet Red outside, the dog was brought in the house but was tied on a leash a good distance away from the child. Again, Cindy watched her mother pet the dog, showing (rather than just telling) the youngster that she had nothing to fear. After every visit, Cindy was praised for getting over her fear and the child always got to do something fun at her aunt's house or on the way home. As you can guess, the final steps brought Cindy physically still closer to Red. Rather than watching Red from across a room, Cindy was asked to move progressively closer to the dog as she watched her mother petting it. Finally, when she was able to do this easily, mother invited Cindy to actually join her in touching the leashed dog. Offering words of encouragement, Mom guided Cindy's hand as she praised the child's fearlessness. If Cindy backed away in fright, she was immediately encouraged to move right back and make friends with the dog again. As always, the episode ended on a positive note, with Cindy receiving strong recognition for her efforts.

Once Cindy was able to approach and pet Red without fear and had grown accustomed to doing this, we asked her mother to arrange for Cindy to meet several other friendly neighborhood dogs in order to ensure that the child had lost her terror of dogs in general and not only of Red. As we expected, much less was required for Cindy to overcome her fear of other dogs once she had been successful with Red. The only remaining task was to tell Cindy that while there is no reason to be afraid of every animal, not all dogs are as friendly as Red and the others. It is most important to remind any child (1) never to approach or pet any dog without first asking the parent whether it is safe to do so, (2) never to tease or hit any dog, even if it is usually friendly, and (3) always to leave a dog alone if it growls or barks. Our aim is to help a child reach that middle ground of being neither terrorized by all animals nor so fearless that animals are approached incautiously.

OVERCOMING THE FEAR OF DOCTORS
AND HOSPITALS

We've now discussed ways to reduce your child's fear of the dark, fear of sleeping alone at night, and fear of friendly animals. In each of these examples, the youngster is afraid of something that is not actually going to hurt him; that's why the fear is unrealistic. There are times, however, when kids develop fears of things that do really hurt them. Trips to the doctor or to the hospital can involve discomfort to a child; once he or she has learned this, those trips can frighten the youngster and provoke behavior problems.

No one looks forward to the possibility of having something done to them that might hurt, and the sheer unfamiliarity of being in a place full of unusual machines, smells, and people can cause emotional discomfort for adults as well as kids. But the critical difference between adults and children is that adults can generally convince themselves that going through something unpleasant is necessary to their overall well-being. We'll grudgingly tolerate getting a shot to prevent the flu or some other illness, and we will consent to the short-term unpleasantness of an operation because it improves our health afterward. Young children do not yet have the experience or thinking capabilities to understand such relationships, and this factor can make routine visits to the doctor, let alone hospital stays, the source of considerable fear.

In theory, our principle of Progressive Exposure should be an effective way to reduce a child's fear of the doctor. If a child goes to the doctor's office or the hospital on a number of occasions and nice things always happen, if the child develops familiarity with what will take place there and if the youngster is never hurt, fears will naturally subside. That's the principle behind Progressive Exposure as we applied it to other kinds of fears. However, it is more difficult and less practical to arrange this kind of gradual exposure for doctor and hospital visits which usually happen only in cases of actual need for treatment. Still, there are a number of steps we can take to help our children overcome fears of the doctor, the dentist, and even of hospital stays.

Never, never lie to your child about going to the doctor and don't spring surprise visits to the doctor or hospital on your child. As we mentioned earlier, don't tell a child something won't hurt at all if it will. You can, on the other hand, acknowledge that something might not be a lot of fun without dwelling on the negative aspects of it. Be sure to convey confidence that your child will be able to handle the situation well, that any discomfort won't last long, and take time to explain how you have handled similar past experiences yourself. The latter point will put your child at ease by allowing him or her to identify with your experiences. Gear this preliminary discussion to the situation your child will face; a visit to the doctor for a routine shot doesn't require as much explanation as a one-week hospital stay.

One of the best examples of what parents should not do comes from the experiences of one of my colleagues. This man, now in his thirties, still recalls his first trip to the hospital as a young child. Although he was found to need minor surgery, his parents did not share that information with him and kept the whole matter a secret. On the day he was scheduled to check into the hospital, his parents told him they were all going on a trip to the local shopping center. Instead of the store, the child found himself being taken to the hospital. To the parents, this probably seemed like a reasonable strategy to save the child worry in anticipation of the hospitalization (and save the parents from having to respond to the child's worried behavior). But the cost of this dishonesty was high: even now, nearly thirty years later, the man still recalls the episode with lingering bitterness. If the parents had explained what would happen in terms he could have understood, they still might have had to deal with some short-term fear, but they would have earned respect for their honesty.

Explain to your child why a trip to the doctor or hospital is needed. Beyond telling a child what will happen when he goes to the doctor or hospital, it is important to explain why the visit is necessary. A child who is extremely fearful of shots should be told they are needed because without them he could get very sick. The parents love the child and do not want this to happen.

Give your child some strategies that he can use to lessen his own fear. Most of us, when we are in situations that cause major fear or discomfort, develop little strategies to calm ourselves. We learn to think about pleasant and relaxing things; sometimes we purposely try to act relaxed by breathing slowly and relaxing our muscles to counter our tension. We often tell ourselves positive things like "Stay calm," "I can handle this," or "I'll be brave" so that we can handle difficult situations more easily. We replace worried thinking with positive thinking. You can help your child do the same thing. When children are old enough to describe why they are afraid of the doctor, dentist, or hospital (and this is usually around the age of five), they are also old enough to benefit from some basic fear control strategies. If your youngster is seriously afraid of something that will happen at the doctor's office, tell him that he will feel much less frightened if he follows these tips:

- Don't think about what you are afraid of. Instead, imagine that you are doing something enjoyable, or that you are someplace that you like. Let your mind wander to pleasant thoughts (like being at a ballgame or at a park).
- Stay calm by breathing slowly and deeply. This helps you to relax.
- Think of how someone you like, someone who is older and brave, would act in that situation. Imagine that you are that person and do the best you can to act just the way you think that person would.
- Silently tell yourself such things as "Be calm," "Just relax," "This won't last long," "I'm a big boy [or girl],"

and so on. If you tell yourself to be unafraid, you will actually feel less fear than when you talk to yourself about being worried.

Interestingly, children who are taught to follow these fear-reducing steps not only feel more relaxed but also experience less physical discomfort even during painful procedures. Dr. Barbara Melamed at the University of Florida has extensively and successfully used this kind of instruction to reduce the anxieties of fearful children scheduled for trips to the dentist and the even greater stress of hospital stays. At our own medical center, children about to undergo the highly stressful procedure of heart catheterization receive specific practice in these ways to reduce their fear.

As you might suspect, simply telling your child to follow certain fear-reducing steps is not nearly as effective as helping your child actually practice them before he faces the dreaded situation. Shortly before the next doctor or hospital visit, pick a quiet time to sit down with your child, explaining each of the techniques we just mentioned and telling the youngster why they will help him feel less fearful. As you do this, encourage your child to show you how he will use the technique; have him demonstrate how he will breathe, have him tell you out loud what he will be saying to himself to reduce fear, have the child tell you who is the brave person he will try to model his conduct after and how he will act, and so on. Then, urge your child to really do all these things in the midst of the feared situation. Remind him again to use these strategies just before the event takes place. Afterward, be sure to discuss with the youngster how the techniques helped.

Try to expose your child to the doctor or hospital on occasions when nothing painful will take place. A major element of fear is the unknown. To the extent that we become familiar with what frightens us, our fear will start to lessen. You can help your child become more at ease by exposing him to the doctor or to the hospital in which he will later be staying. In the case of the doctor, allow your child to go with you (or with older brothers or sisters) when routine office visits are made. This will permit the youngster to become familiar with and more at ease in the doctor's office surroundings. Make it a point to introduce your fearful child to the doctor or nurse, even when another child is actually there for an appointment. This will allow your child to get to know (and we hope to like) the people he will encounter on his own later visits. By all means let both the physician and the office staff know that you are trying to help your child overcome a fear of the doctor; good pediatricians will go to special lengths in order to put fearful children at ease, and may conduct little tours of the office to familiarize children with it.

Hospital stays are more threatening to children than are visits to the doctor. In a child's eyes the hospital is a huge, intimidating place. What goes on there is mysterious to the child, and the parent may not be physically with the youngster during parts of the stay. Hospitals recognize how common children's fears are, and many have developed special programs to help children understand what will happen to them once they begin their stay. These programs might include taking the youngster who will later be a patient on a guided tour of the hospital, introducing the child to various hospital staff he will later see, showing the child special videotape films that explain common medical procedures, and otherwise making the upcoming hospital stay less frightening. If your child will be going to the hospital, be sure to check with your doctor to see whether your hospital offers such a program. Many do.

Even if your hospital does not yet have such a formal orientation program, you may be able to accomplish some of these goals on your own. As a first step, prepare your child for his stay by explaining the kinds of things that will happen to him there. If an operation is involved, you can describe how the child will be given a shot, taken to another room and asked to breathe something that will make him sleepy, and so on. Your pediatrician can — and should — help you by explaining the same points to the child. By all means keep your explanations simple enough for your child to understand and present them in a positive tone, making the occasion more like an upcoming adventure than something to be feared.

Consider the possibility of rooming-in arrangements so that you can spend more time with your child during the hospital stay. While hospitals traditionally have visiting hours, many doctors recognize that children need more reassuring contact with their parents than short visiting hours allow. If your youngster is extremely fearful, it will be comforting if you plan to spend as much time with him as possible. It will also make you feel better. If this arrangement is feasible for you, discuss with your physician whether you can spend up to the entire day and evening with your child during his stay. Some hospitals have developed rooming-in plans in which parents can actually share a hospital room with their children. If your child's hospitalization will be reasonably brief, if you would feel better rooming-in with the youngster, and if your child's fears would be lessened by your presence, this arrangement should be investigated.

With the right planning and preparation before a hospital stay, many sources of fear can be reduced. While almost no children (or adults) like hospital visits, a child's terror of them can be eliminated.

8/

Promoting Your
Child's Self-Expression

BEING a parent requires dealing with the kinds of everyday challenges and behavior problems we've described throughout this book. These are the daily tasks that confront parents of all young children. It's important, however, to think beyond your child's current behavior problems to the longer-range qualities and competencies you would like to see him or her develop and maintain through life. Being able to make decisions on one's own and to express individual views or feelings to others are qualities we hope our children will acquire. Just as parents are in a position to solve a child's everyday behavior problems, they are also in a position to help their children begin to develop lasting and positive skills.

Although we usually think of decision-making and individualism as adult characteristics, they begin to appear quite early in life and they can be developed into positive attributes. While personality style and values can undergo change during a lifetime, early childhood experiences can shape the general direction of a person's later values and skill development. In this chapter we will turn our attention to some early-life learning experiences that can contribute to your child's personality development.

HELPING YOUR CHILD LEARN TO
MAKE DECISIONS

In adolescence and adulthood we are called upon to reach decisions, both small and large ones, almost all of the time. Those who have refined the skill of thinking through problems and arriving at sound solutions have gained an important asset for living. These are the individuals who can solve their own everyday problems and dilemmas, think for themselves, and achieve success in their relationships and their careers. Adults who lack decision-making skills often feel victimized by circumstances and trapped by problems they have been unable to resolve. Clearly, decision-making is an ability we hope our children will develop.

It is useful to think of the ability to make decisions as a skill. By skill we mean that decision-making is a characteristic that people are not born with but instead must gradually develop, practice, and refine. In order to be the kind of adult who can confidently make large decisions, it is necessary to have the experience of making small decisions earlier in life. Thus, the skill of decision-making can best be developed through practice, beginning in childhood and continuing as the person matures. Keep in mind that your child's age determines the complexity of the decisions he or she can make. Three- and four-year-olds don't yet have the reasoning skills needed to weigh complex alternatives to problems, but they can respond to simple decision-making questions (such as "What crayon color do you want to make the house?"). Children of five and six are generally more able to think of alternatives or solutions on their own.

There is an almost natural tendency for parents not to encourage their children to actively participate in making decisions, and this seems especially true for the parents of young children. It probably comes about for two reasons. First, parents are often unaware that four-, five-, or six-year-old children can make many decisions about matters affecting them. A second reason is convenience: It is much easier and quicker to tell a child what to do than it is to sit down and help the youngster make his own choices.

Helping your child learn to make decisions may involve changing the way you now interact with him or her. Let's look at the way everyday situations present the opportunity for a child to make decisions to see what a parent can do to foster this skill.

"Mom, I'm bored. What should I do?" Many parents hear this from their kids, especially on rainy days or whenever the youngster's usual activities are unavailable (perhaps when a favorite playmate is away on vacation). The parent's usual response is to decide for the youngster and to tell the child what to do — "Go outside and play," "Why don't you go pick up your toys in the den?," or "Why don't you play with one of the toys you got for Christmas?" While this solves the immediate question of what the child will do, the youngster has not learned how to decide what he wants to do to occupy his time and an opportunity to practice some early decision-making has been missed. Parents can actively help their kids learn to decide such matters by taking the approach illustrated below:

Child: "Mom, I'm bored. What's there to do?

Parent: "That depends on what you want to do. What are some things you could do today?"

Child: "I don't know. Watch TV, I guess."

Parent: "That's one thing, but I bet you can think of some others."

Child: "Well ... I could play with the talking robot game, or else I could go over to Charlie's house."

Parent: "Good. You thought of three different things. You could watch TV, play with the robot game, or go see Charlie next door. Which do you want to do?"

Child: "I think I'll go to Charlie's now and watch TV later."

Parent: "That sounds like a good idea. I'm glad you decided for yourself."

In this conversation the parent helped her child make his own decision by following two basic steps: by first asking the youngster to think of several possible courses of action, and then by asking the youngster to weigh the alternatives and decide which one would be best. The mother avoided telling her child what to do. This two-step process is the essence of decision-making. It's the way most adults arrive at major decisions, such as whether to accept a new job or whether to move, and smaller decisions, such as how to spend an evening or who to invite to a party. We think first of the alternatives open to us and then evaluate which one best meets our needs. Many everyday opportunities arise in which kids can make their own decisions or help you arrive at some decision that involves them. Your job as a parent is to recognize when these opportunities occur and guide your child into thinking of solutions on his own.

One way to assist your child in making decisions is by asking the youngster to offer his opinion or choice in matters that affect him. If the family is going out to dinner and you aren't sure where you want to go, encourage your child to offer his opinion. When it's time to set out school clothes to wear the next day, let your child help pick the outfit to be worn. If it's a Saturday afternoon and you want to go somewhere with the child, invite him to help decide what to do. The idea is to allow your youngster to practice making decisions by actively soliciting the child's opinions and suggestions in matters that affect him.

Keep in mind that any young child will occasionally need your patient guidance in learning how to make decisions. Children can't always identify various options and they often lack the experience to know which choice will turn out best. Part of your job is to help teach your youngster the consequences of his decisions, as we show in the following example.

"I don't want to go to the doctor." In earlier chapters we discussed how to handle children's fears and noncompliance with reasonable requests. It is also possible for parents to help their children understand decisions that are in children's best interests. Five-year-old Tammy wants to go to a summer day-camp sponsored by her church. In order to attend camp every child must first get a checkup and a tetanus shot, and Tammy hates shots. Tammy's mother agrees that day-camp would be a nice experience and wants her daughter to go, even if it means dragging her to the doctor's office for the required shot and checkup. But does Mom have to resort to force? Let's listen in on a conversation the two could have in which Tammy could come to understand why the visit to the doctor is needed:

Tammy: "I don't want to go to the doctor."

Mother: "I understand that Tammy, I really do. Nobody likes to go to doctors very much, even me. But the camp says you have to do that if you want to join in. Isn't that right?"

Tammy: "Yes, but I still don't want to get the shot."

Mother: "I'd like to tell you why it might be important to go. You're saying that you don't want to see the doctor, but what will happen then?"

Tammy: "I can't go to camp."

Mother: "That's right. Do you want to miss camp?"

Tammy: "No — I want to go to camp."

Mother: "What's the other choice?"

Tammy: "Going to the doctor, I guess."

Mother: "Right. If you want to go to camp, where you'll have a lot of fun for two whole weeks, you need to get a quick little shot over with first. I know you don't like shots, but we have to decide if we're willing to give up all that fun at camp just because of one shot that will last only a few seconds. Can you see why the decision to go to the doctor makes sense?"

In this conversation the parent is helping her child learn to think and to arrive at a decision. This mother had to guide the youngster by helping her identify two choices (to go or not to go to the doctor) as well as the consequences of each choice. You can see that the process here is quite different from telling the child "You have to go to the doctor because I say so," which is the response parents sometimes use to handle a child's disagreement with their wishes. Instead of feeling as though she was forced into going to the doctor, the child was given an opportunity to hear, understand, and be included in the parent's decision-making. Being part of a decision reduces the likelihood of further conflict because it is more likely that the child will arrive at the same conclusion the parent has already reached.

When we speak of children's decision-making, it raises the question of what youngsters should be allowed to decide themselves. Everyday choices and preferences — what to do with one's time, what games to play, what clothes to wear — can generally be decided by most children with minimal discussion and guidance from the parent. Making these routine decisions is the skill we want a child to acquire. There are certain other decisions, however, that kids can't be permitted to make. Allowing your child to decide not to go to the doctor, dentist, or hospital isn't reasonable any more than it would be to allow him to decide to play in the middle of the street. These are all situations where a wrong decision would obviously create the potential for harm or violate your own strong wishes. But you can still sit down with your youngster and carefully explain how you arrived at a decision affecting him, allowing the child to think along with you and see how you made the choice. As you do this, you are actually modeling important decision-making skills that your child can later imitate when he eventually has to make choices on his own. Keep in mind that skills, including decision-making, are learned gradually and only with patient guidance. Simply telling a child to decide something for himself is ineffective and will only confuse the youngster; taking a few minutes to discuss a dilemma, review choices, and help your child pick one is the ideal way to teach decision-making.

CHILDREN'S SELF-ESTEEM AND INDIVIDUALITY

One of the truly remarkable things about children is their uniqueness. Each child is different from every other. When we consider the many qualities that make us who we are — our various physical attributes, intellectual abilities, athletic skills, interests, competencies, social styles, likes and dislikes, worries and fears — it becomes clear that every youngster has unique and individual characteristics that together determine his or her personality. The things that make a youngster different from others also make him special. Even among brothers or sisters raised in the same home and close in age, parents often see incredible differences in the way siblings think, feel, and act. One youngster is extraverted while another is shy, one excels in sports while another is studious, one walks and talks early while another does so late, one child wants to stay close to his parent while the other can't run off fast enough. In these and many other ways, children continually present us with evidence of their individual personalties.

One of the questions I am often asked by parents is whether their child has a good self-concept or high self-esteem. Unfortunately, self-esteem is one of those psychological terms that is much easier to use than to define. A major aspect of self-esteem involves whether a person thinks of his skills, competencies, and limitations in a positive or negative way. A child who has had the experience of receiving praise and encouragement for his successes and whose efforts at difficult tasks, even if unsuccessful, were recognized by his parents, is a child who is likely to evaluate himself in positive terms. Children who find themselves criticized, whose successes go unnoticed, or whose parents try to make them into something they are not, come to evaluate themselves negatively and to see themselves as failures, often for many years to come.

From this viewpoint, an important task of parenthood lies in identifying your child's individual pattern of strengths and abilities and then helping your youngster discover and excel in them. As youngsters learn, experience, and hear from parents about what they can do well, their self-concepts become correspondingly more positive and they become confident enough to tackle tasks that previously seemed too difficult. How can parents promote this process? Based on experiences with families in our clinic as well as with the psychological literature on child development, we feel certain guidelines should be followed to encourage children's growth and individuality. Let's consider several.

BE CAREFUL OF "BE PERFECT"

There is nothing that a child starts to do in early life that he is not doing for the first time. Walking, talking, toilet training, playing with others, dressing himself, playing games, playing with friends — these are just a few of the activities kids do for the very first time in early childhood. This fact, which we often overlook, has several implications. The first is that no child, no matter how bright or eager, will be able to do all things well or will be able to do things well the first time he tries them. There will be errors, mistakes, fears, and hesitations in most tasks that a child first attempts. The second implication is that parents, by virtue of the time they spend with their children, are in the position to help them begin to feel competent.

Cecile, who just turned four, was in the den one afternoon playing with some building blocks she had received as a birthday present. After playing intently with them for about fifteen minutes, Cecile called in her mother to look at what she had made. "It's a house!" said the child. In fact, there was only a pile of blocks. Mom watched for a moment and told Cecile that it didn't look much like a house at all.

Jerome is a shy six-year-old who doesn't make friends easily. One Saturday, Jerome's father was outside talking to a neighbor in the front yard when some kids of about Jerome's age came by. Jerome watched but didn't speak to them, even though he was not far away. When the boys had passed, the father turned from his neighbor and angrily said to Jerome, "You're always by yourself; what are you so afraid of?"

In each of these examples a child was made to feel bad in a situation that could have been a positive learning experience, and it was because the parent expected more than the child was able to give. It may be quite a while before Cecile again calls her mother to see something she tried to create, and Jerome will probably be even more self-conscious and uncomfortable the next time kids pass by his house. These parents brought to their children's attention only that they failed at something.

What might Cecile's mother or Jerome's father have done differently? Two things could have made these into positive rather than negative episodes for the children. The first requires that the parent recognize something good in what the child did. Cecile's mother might have complimented her daughter on working to create something imaginative from the blocks; Jerome could have been told that he is a good boy and has lots of qualities other children would like. Second, each parent could use the situation to teach the child how to be more successful in the future. Cecile might have been shown by her Mom how to go about putting blocks together so they do look more like a house. Rather than simply criticizing his son for his shyness, Jerome's dad could have spent a few minutes in private talking with (and showing) his son how to go about greeting other kids.

Our point here is that parents should be careful not to expect perfectly skilled behavior in their children. It is always more helpful to praise something your child did well and then, if need be, to follow this with guidance or practice in how to improve even more.

REINFORCE AND RECOGNIZE YOUR CHILD FOR TRYING, NOT ONLY FOR SUCCEEDING

This principle follows closely from the one we just discussed. Very rarely do people succeed at everything they attempt, and just as rarely are people "the best" in all their pursuits. Most of us aren't the best-known person in our line of work, we weren't the valedictorians in our graduation class, we aren't the best golfer at the course where we play or the most gifted artist in our city. Yet this doesn't prevent us from enjoying our work, studying in school, or developing hobbies and creative interests. We've learned that trying and enjoying are often more important than being the best, and that's what leads us to undertake activities in which we are not totally proficient.

Children need to learn the same thing, and parents can help them develop this attitude. One of the best ways is by recognizing and praising your child's efforts at tasks, apart from whether the efforts were entirely successful. The youngster who worked hard to completely dress herself one day, even if all the buttons ended up in the wrong buttonholes, should be praised for her attempt to get dressed herself. The youngster who falls off his bike, gets on, and falls off again while learning to ride still deserves recognition for his efforts if not yet his success. The girl who becomes frustrated while trying hard to copy printed letters or numbers needs encouragement for attempting, rather than criticism for falling short of perfection.

It's especially important that parents seek out opportunities to recognize their child's efforts in tasks their youngsters are beginning to learn or those that are now difficult for the child. This bolsters confidence and helps a youngster become more willing to undertake new challenges. While kids won't become the best at everything they try, they can learn the important lesson that their efforts count and will still be recognized.

AVOID COMPARING YOUR CHILD, POSITIVELY OR NEGATIVELY, WITH OTHERS

"Why can't you act as good as your sister Dorothy?" "Billy next door never gets all his clothes messed up when he goes out to play." "I wish you could play ball as well as Jim did in that game." These kinds of statements can be extremely destructive to a child's sense of competence because they convey that the youngster isn't as good as someone he or she knows, and they further imply that the parent likes the other child better. Even when a parent is angry or disappointed, negative comparisons to another child (whether that child is a friend, neighbor, brother or sister) create many more problems than they solve.

Respond to your child's conduct on its own merit. If your child seriously misbehaves, by all means handle that misbehavior, but do it directly and without commenting that some other child wouldn't act so badly. And if your child attempts something but does poorly at it, remember the importance of recognizing individual effort rather than noticing only success. Because children aren't all alike, they won't be equally good in the same activities.

I also advise parents to avoid making positive comparisons of a child's conduct with that of others. When a youngster does something well, it is desirable that this receive attention and be reinforced. It isn't good, however, to convey that the child is much better at what he did than someone else might be. Just as a child shouldn't hear that he is worse in some task, skill, or ability than his brother or cousin, it isn't necessary to say that he is better. Positive recognition of a child's efforts lead to self-confidence and good self-appraisal; comparisons that convey "betterness" may encourage undesirable notions of superiority and conceit.

YOUR CHILD'S STRENGTHS AREN'T NECESSARILY THE SAME AS YOURS

As parents raise children, it is very natural for them to recall their own early-life experiences and use these recollections to guide their children. Parents sometimes recall their own childhoods, remembering their hobbies, interests, failures, successes, and ways of getting along with others, and from this personal experience base help their kids handle similar situations. Even when parents don't consciously try to do this, they still model specific interests, values, and skills that their youngsters will often learn to imitate. The process of helping your child handle life situations by relying on (and teaching from) your own experiences is a very useful process. It allows the youngster to hear or see how you once handled a problem that he now also has, and children learn positive basic living skills and values from their parents.

Up to this point we have stressed that parents and their kids tend to have a good deal in common. Personality, social style, intellectual ability, and values all tend to be at least moderately correlated between parents and their children. But in spite of whatever similarities exist, there are also going to be important differences. Parents have the responsibility to help youngsters develop their own interests and abilities, even if they differ from those of the parents.

Margaret is an outgoing and active child who loves to do things outside. She's especially good at sports, games that involve a lot of running and jumping, and she already loves to play basketball. Margaret's mother, who is a more traditional and quiet housewife, would really prefer to see her child be less sports-minded and more interested in learning to cook and acquire domestic skills.

Brad's father was a successful athlete throughout his school years, starring in football, baseball, and track. He really looked forward to having a son who could learn to do all the things he had done so well in his school years. However, Brad is a small child who just doesn't seem to have his father's athletic ability and coordination. Brad would much rather work on puzzles, play table games with his friends, and collect coins.

These children have interests and skills unlike those of their parents. Parents can, of course, try to force their children to develop interests more consistent with their own wishes: Margaret's mother could make her child act more "ladylike" and Brad's father could drag the boy, if need be, to a Little League baseball game. An alternative approach is for the parent simply to recognize and appreciate that children can be different from their parents, and help develop those skills and interests the child does have. Too many youngsters are made to feel like disappointments simply because they have skills, competencies, or interests different from those of their parents. So although you can encourage a youngster to try activities you once enjoyed, be careful not to force a narrow set of specific interests on your child. Let — and help — your youngster develop his own.

"BOYS DON'T . . . ," "GIRLS SHOULDN'T . . .": SEX-ROLE STEREOTYPES THAT CAN LIMIT GROWTH

Not too long ago everybody "knew" that boys were always expected to be big and strong, athletic, competitive, forceful, and leaders among their peers. They weren't supposed to show tender emotion, cry, or be afraid of anything. Girls were expected to be dainty, noncompetitive, unathletic, and supportive. Boys were encouraged to become doctors, lawyers, carpenters, or engineers when they grow up, while girls (in the event it might be necessary for them to work) were encouraged to become teachers or nurses. For many years these widely held expectations determined the conduct, social roles, and aspirations of boys and girls; for this reason they constitute what we call sex-role stereotypes. Most of us, to a greater or lesser degree, grew up with such stereotypes affecting our own behavior. Perhaps as much as the rest of society, psychologists and psychiatrists shared these beliefs and felt the well-adjusted boy was one who identified closely only with traditionally masculine characteristics and that emotionally healthy girls identified with a stereotyped feminine role.

Happily, both professionals and parents are now questioning and rejecting some of the traditionally held assumptions about sex-role stereotypes and adjustment. We are now realizing that the person (whether a male or a female) who is well-adjusted is one who has many ways of handling life situations, many different skills, and many interests. It's good for boys to be athletic, strong, and leaders — but it's also good for them to be sensitive, gentle, and capable of showing emotion. There is nothing wrong with girls choosing traditionally feminine interests and characteristics — as long as they don't feel it's wrong to be assertive and competitive when these traits are called for.

Cornell University psychologist Sandra Bem has extensively studied the relationship between sex-role stereotypes and mental health, concluding that the most flexible and adjusted individuals are those who have the skills to do whatever is needed in a particular situation, even when this differs from traditional role stereotypes. Girls who grow up thinking that it is wrong to assert their opinions, make decisions, or achieve success in sports have a more restricted range of living skills than those who learn that these are valued characteristics for people, regardless of sex. Boys who are led to believe it is somehow unmanly to feel and express sympathy, tenderness, and emotion have a similarly limited range of living skills, and aren't going to know how to act in situations where these are the characteristics that are needed. In support of this notion, Bem and other researchers have found that both men and women with highly sex-stereotyped personalities are lower in self-esteem than persons who do not have such a restricted view of what is appropriate for males and females. Parents should remain sensitive to the limiting effects of rigid sex-role stereotyping of children. Instead of reinforcing these stereotypes, they need to encourage their youngsters to develop effective living skills.

Be cautious of telling your child that "boys don't . . ." or "girls shouldn't . . ." It is reasonable for boy and girls to develop play activities and habits that will lead to peer acceptance. For example, the boy who plays exclusively with dolls or cooking toys may receive ridicule and embarrassment from others.

Nevertheless, some parents become far too restrictive concerning the characteristics their children should develop. The boy who cries when a pet dies or the girl who tells her parents that she wants to grow up to become a doctor are expressing positive feelings and aspirations. Responding to these actions by saying that it is not right for boys to cry or girls to have such career goals reinforces negative sex-role stereotyping and limits the child's potential. Be encouraging of behavior, values, and interests that you feel are good human characteristics, regardless of whether they might be traditionally masculine or feminine.

Because children model characteristics seen in their parents, your own actions will influence your child's views of acceptable behavior. When kids see firsthand that a good Mom can be someone who is not only affectionate, warm, and loving, but also competent, successful, and achievement-oriented, they learn that this blend of characteristics constitutes a positive role for women. Boys whose fathers are seen as affectionate, warm, and sensitive are more likely to permit these characteristics in themselves. Although parents are certainly not the only models who influence the style and attitudes of their children, they are the primary ones, especially for younger kids. To the extent that your own conduct reflects non-sex-stereotyped values and interests, your child will be exposed to this role model.

Notice and reinforce your child for displaying characteristics you would like to see developed. As we have stressed throughout this book, the best way to promote desirable actions in children is to reinforce those behaviors. This principle applies not only to specific behavior problems but also to the development of compassion, kindness, sensitivity, assertiveness, and achievement. For example, if you feel that it is important for your boy to develop a more compassionate attitude, make a real effort to notice when the child displays kindness toward others and convey your pride in his conduct. Girls can learn to develop important skills like assertiveness and decision-making that have not historically been part of the stereotyped feminine role when their parents provide opportunities for them to practice those competencies.

In summary, the process of raising children requires that parents develop strategies for handling and solving youngsters' everyday behavior problems. Although solving problems is one part of a parent's role, it is also important to facilitate learning experiences that will foster the development of a child's individuality, decision-making skills, and positive self-concept.

9/
Your Child's First Days Away from Home

BREAKING away from parents and family is an inevitable part of growing up for all children. There are a number of milestones and separations that children and their parents will pass through, starting in childhood and ending much later in life. In early childhood they include the first time a child's parents go on a trip without him, the time when a youngster starts in daycare because his parents work, or the time when a child first spends the night at a friend's house. Beginning school is particularly important because the youngster is not only on his own and away from home every day but is also embarking on his new role as a student. The first date, school graduation, and even later, moving away from home, getting married and establishing one's own family — each event represents part of the continuing growth process toward establishing independence. This process begins quite early in a child's life, even though it is often difficult for parents to admit that their child is really starting to grow up. (In retrospect, helping your child establish his independence and maturity becomes one of the greatest joys and satisfactions of parenthood.)

As with other new experiences in your child's life, each step of the breaking-away process can go smoothly or certain problems may develop. Sometimes children become fearful and exhibit behavior problems when their parents leave them, even if it is only for a short vacation the parents want to take by themselves or when it's time for the child to start going to school.

Sometimes parents, as well, feel uncertain (and guilty) as it becomes time for their child to strike out more on his own, especially when the youngster objects to being away from them.

There are three periods during which a young child may particularly need to function apart from his family. These are when a child attends day-care or nursery school, when he starts elementary school for the first time, and when he begins to make friends on his own. In this chapter we will discuss some issues a parent should consider when a child reaches each of these breaking-away points.

WHAT PARENTS SHOULD KNOW
ABOUT DAY-CARE

The popular stereotype of families in the good old days had the father going off to work every morning and the mother staying at home with her child until the youngster reached the age of six, at which point he also left every morning, but for school. Even with her child at school, a dedicated mother continued to stay at home all day, doing the housekeeping, being available should any problem at school come up, and having cookies and milk ready for the youngster when school was over. Although good fathers usually worked, good mothers usually didn't, and neighbors or relatives might look askance at any family with such dire financial problems that they would even have to consider day-care for a child in order that both parents could work. This family stereotype isn't accurate now; in fact it wasn't all that accurate even in the past. There have always been a number of single-parent families, families in which both parents had to work, and families in which both parents chose to work. There have always been children in some form of day-care, even though the number of formal day-care centers or nursery schools was much smaller in the past. And while there weren't many early studies in this area, children whose parents both worked didn't seem to have any more or any fewer adjustment problems than those who were raised by a parent who was at home throughout their childhood.

That, however, is not to say that children don't need a great deal of close contact with their parents early in life. One of the most critical events that occurs in infancy is called bonding. As its name implies, bonding refers to the emotional attachment that must develop between an infant and the mother very early in life. Being held, cuddled and gently rocked, softly spoken to, and simply gazing into the mother's face and seeing her gaze back are all early-life experiences that help bond or attach the infant to the mother. Studies now suggest that this is a gradual process that occurs early in the first year of an infant's life, usually over the first two months. Children who tragically lose their mother at birth as a result of her death or some totally incapacitating illness that removes her during that critical bonding period seem more prone to experience emotional problems later in life. Providing plenty of close nurturant contact — both physical and emotional — with the mother during early infancy is one of the most important first jobs that parents face.

IS DAY-CARE GOOD OR BAD FOR CHILDREN?

A whole range of child-care options is now available to the parents of children who have not yet reached school age. Which of these options you choose depends primarily on your own life-style and values or attitudes. You might, for example, decide to be a full-time mother, staying home with your youngster until he reaches school age while Dad goes to work; you might decide that your youngster will be raised by a full-time father, in which arrangement Mom goes off to work while Dad stays home with the kids; you might decide that your child will attend day-care so that both parents can work or because yours is a one-parent family and there would be no one home with your child during working hours; or you might decide to arrange for child care not at a formal day-care center but with someone coming into your home (or your child going to theirs) each day.

A number of recent studies have examined the intellectual development and emotional adjustment of pre-school-age children who go to high-quality day-care versus those who are raised with a parent — either the mother or the father — at home all day. For the most part few consistent differences between day-care and parent-at-home children have been found. Instead, it seems that what works best depends on the attitudes and needs of the whole family. If a parent finds it more rewarding or fulfilling to stay at home, and if family financial circumstances permit it, then by all means the parent should do just that. On the other hand, a parent certainly need not feel guilty if, either by choice or necessity, a decision is made that the child will attend day-care while the parent works. Happily, we've begun to realize that while raising a child is a challenge, a time-consuming task, and a tremendous source of satisfaction, it shouldn't be the only challenge, task, or satisfaction in any parent's life.

Quite often in my own practice, I talk with parents who feel guilty because they somehow think that being a good parent means that you must devote one hundred percent of your waking time to your child. Usually, because of traditional sex-role stereotypes, it is the mother who feels this conflict between being a good parent and doing other gratifying things with her life. My advice to these parents is pretty straightforward: Caring parenthood, at least once your child is past early infancy, is not incompatible with other daytime activities such as working. And if working full time takes you away from your child more than you want, work only part time if that is feasible. It is undoubtedly far worse for a child to be raised by a resentful parent who stays home but would rather not, than for that youngster to be in day-care some of the time and have the benefit of a satisfied, fulfilled parent when both get together at the day's end. The decision about day-care, then, is a choice that must take into account your needs, satisfactions, and attitudes about how you want to spend your time as well as your views on being a parent. There is no clear-cut right or wrong thing to do.

If your child does attend day-care or nursery school, you do have some special things to consider. One is making certain that your child benefits fully from the time he does spend at home with you; another is choosing a good day-care program that meets your child's needs.

IT'S THE QUALITY OF TIME WITH YOUR CHILD (MORE THAN QUANTITY) THAT COUNTS

Let's consider two hypothetical families, the Bakers and the Petersons. Each family has a four-year-old girl. Mrs. Baker spends her whole day at home with her child. Her daughter, after breakfast, watches television most of the morning while Mom goes about her housework. The child's afternoons are spent outside if the weather's nice or inside playing a game by herself or watching more TV if the weather's bad. If we were to observe Mrs. Baker and her daughter, we would find that they actually spend very little time talking or playing or doing things together. Most of their conversation consists of Mrs. Baker's directions: "Honey, go outside and play," "It's time for lunch," or "Let's take a nap." Although Mrs. Baker is spending a lot of time physically near her youngster, the daughter is receiving very little of her mother's attention.

Mrs. Peterson's daughter goes off to day-care when her Mom goes to work each weekday morning. But in the afternoon, Mrs. Peterson always spends a good deal of time talking and actively interacting with her daughter. Mom plans it this way, because although she works, she wants to reserve some special times each afternoon or evening to share with the child. Some afternoons they go for a walk together at a park near their home. Mrs. Peterson makes it a point to talk with her daughter to find out about the things the child did at nursery school that day. And Mrs. Peterson always lets her daughter play grown up by having the child help set the table and assist a bit with dinner.

Certainly, most parents who stay at home with their children are not as inattentive and removed from them as Mrs. Baker, nor are all working parents as dedicated to arranging special times with their child as Mrs. Peterson. But it is clear from our descriptions of these two hypothetical families that Mrs. Peterson's daughter, who spends less time with her mom each day, actually gets more from the times they are together. Within limits, it is the quality of time together, rather than the number of hours, that is critical to a child's emotional development and feelings of security. While quality of time spent together is an issue that applies to all parents, it is especially important for the family whose child is gone during the day. Make it a point, after your day at work and your child's day in preschool, to set aside some time for special activities that bring the family close together. Don't try to create entertaining extravaganzas for your child; after a day's work you probably won't have the energy to follow through on plans that are too demanding. Instead, a game of catch, a walk to the park, playing a game your child enjoys, romping with the dog, and just spending some time showing interest in your youngster's daily activities are all examples of everyday things that enhance the quality of your child's time with you and permit you to have positive feelings about yourself as a working parent.

HOW TO CHOOSE A DAY-CARE OR PRESCHOOL CENTER

When you pick a day-care or preschool program for your three- or four-year-old, you are in fact selecting the people to whom you will entrust the care of your child when you're not present. As we might expect, the programs offered by day-care and preschool centers vary greatly; some are of marginal quality while others provide extremely high-level educational and social experiences for the children who attend. It's important, therefore, to know how to find the best programs in your area. Here are some ways to go about it:

1. *Check with your neighbors and coworkers who have preschool-age children in day-care.* Find out from them the names of the day-care centers their children attend. Another good source are parents whose children attend church school with yours and Sunday school teachers themselves. Ask parents how satisfied they are with the programs their children attend. What do the children do all day at the center? Do the staff communicate regularly with parents, either formally (in some kind of report) or informally (in conversations with the parent when a child is being picked up)? Does your neighbor's or friend's child like to go to day-care (and if so, why does he like to go), or does the child not want to go (and if that's the case, why doesn't he)? Start your search, then, by learning what experiences other parents have had with various centers.

See whether you can get an elementary school teacher to recommend local preschool programs. Elementary school teachers, especially kindergarten and first-grade teachers, see a lot of children who've been in various day-care programs before starting elementary school and can give you solid advice about which local programs appear to be the best. Also, because both preschool staff and elementary school teachers share an interest in young children, teachers often know many local day-care staff on a personal and professional basis. Again, this helps them provide knowledgable recommendations. While the public school itself probably won't provide you with an official recommendation, an individual elementary school teacher often will give you good advice.

2. *Consider the locations and costs of programs you are evaluating.* Obviously, geography will play a part in your se-

lection, because the center you choose must be relatively close to your home and your work. Nothing is worse than fighting your way through traffic to the other side of town to pick up your youngster after you're tired from a day at work. Convenience counts. Cost counts too, although not as much as you might expect. In general, day-care programs offered by churches, universities or colleges, and other nonprofit groups are less expensive than those offered by commercial day-care centers. On the other hand, commercial day-care centers may have better access to specialized educational resources (games, audiovisual learning aids, and the like) and staff training programs than do some smaller centers. Keep in mind, however, that child care made necessary because a parent works is a deductible expense on your income tax return. This may narrow the cost difference between programs that charge less and those that charge more.

3. When you've developed your list of potential centers, plan to visit each one you're considering. Arrange to see a preschool center at least once when children are there and daily activities are taking place. Allow yourself plenty of time to talk with the center's director, and even more important, to observe what is taking place throughout the center. This will give you an opportunity to watch firsthand what the children (and the staff) are actually doing.

A very good time to visit is midway through the afternoon. Any center can look good early in the morning, but the truly well-organized and clean center should still look respectable — especially the bathrooms, lunch room, and play areas — after they have been used during the day. Don't expect everything to be entirely tidy after a day's use; it won't be, given the way children play. But do expect the lunchroom to be clean shortly after it has been used, the bathrooms to be neat and in good condition, any trash to be removed, the floors to be clean, and so on. If they're not, it suggests too few staff for the number of children attending the program, or a staff that doesn't like to do the routine cleaning up that is essential in any day-care program.

On your visit, there are some specific questions to ask and some specific things to observe:

What is the staff-to-child ratio? For children three to five years old, look for a ratio of about one staff person for each six to seven children. For younger children, the ratio should be higher, with one staff person for each four to five children. Be sure that only employees who really provide care for the children are counted in the staff ratio you are given.

What are the staff's qualifications? At a good center, the upper-level staff (director and teachers) will have formal training and educational degrees in child development, elementary education, early child education, or in similar areas. Ask about the exact qualifications of the higher-level staff, especially those who oversee educational plans. But don't expect all staff to have formal degrees; very few preschools could afford to operate if every employee was required to have a college degree in education. However, staff such as preschool aides should be experienced and have had some formal training in child care. Again, don't be shy about asking such questions.

Does the center meet health, fire, and other safety codes? Most states and cities have codes governing the safety and health standards for day-care and preschool centers. Ask whether the center you are visiting meets all of these codes. Later, call the city or state agency that oversees them to double-check on the center's certification and any record of complaints or failed inspections.

How is television used in the center's program? Although there are some very good programs on television that can be incorporated into a preschool's educational curriculum, television can also be misused as a pacifier. If a center allows its youngsters to sit and watch TV for hours, more beneficial activities aren't taking place. Also, ask (and then watch to see) what programs are being watched. If *General Hospital, As the World Turns,* game shows, or movies are on, the staff may be more interested in their own entertainment than in your child's activities.

How well are educational programs carried out? Day-care and preschool are not (and shouldn't be) as educationally structured as later elementary school will be. By the same token, a youngster's time in a center should include activities and learning games appropriate for the child's age. These might include activities, like arts or crafts, that refine perceptual-motor skills; games that teach children their colors, numbers, or letters, and develop attention span; physical activities to improve coordination; or tasks that promote social cooperation with other children. The exact program your child will encounter depends on your child's age, the philosophy of the center, and the center's resources. A wise parent will find out as much as possible about the specific educational development program offered by each center being considered. Ask to see (or, if it's not in written form, ask to be told) the typical day's schedule for a child of your youngster's age.

How do day-care staff actually spend their time? When you're observing the activities at the center, pay special attention to the actions of the staff. In a good program, all the staff will spend more time interacting with children than with each other. If you see staff actively engaged with and attentive to the youngsters, it's a sign that they really care about and enjoy their work. The best way to find out whether this is the case is by watching what goes on in the room.

Who at the center is trained in first aid? A number of staff should have received formal first aid training so they can handle any accidents or injuries that might occur.

Beware of long nap times. Children, especialy young ones, do need occasional naps. Most day-care and preschool programs have rest times, but be certain these do not occur too often or for long periods during the day. A good program will schedule activities to keep children active rather than encouraging them to sleep.

As you can see, selecting a day-care program for your child involves a fair amount of questioning, information gathering, and personal observation. It is important that a parent take plenty of time to sit in a corner of the center and simply watch what goes on. Any good center will let you do this, and if you want to observe further, will invite you to come back. If you find that the center earns good marks in all the areas we've mentioned, and if you also feel intuitively that the staff has a warm and effective approach toward children, you've probably found a center to which you can entrust your youngster.

IT'S TIME FOR MY CHILD TO START SCHOOL... BUT HE WON'T GO

One of the most important events in the lives of most five-year-olds is starting school. For some children, this is the first time they will routinely spend their days away from home, away from family, and in a largely unfamiliar environment. Even for children who are already accustomed to being away from home (such as those who have been in day-care while their parents work), school is still a new experience because it now carries a unique purpose: to learn. Learning in school obviously includes educational studies, but what kids learn there extends far beyond reading, writing, spelling, and science. It is here that they also develop the skills to get along and make friends with other children, to interact with adults other than family members, to follow directions and ask questions, to solve problems, and to function in a setting in which they are not under their parents' watchful eyes.

When people enter novel situations and don't have a great

deal of experience to guide their conduct, they may encounter some problems in adapting to the new environment. When you first started school, began your first job, or moved to a new city, it undoubtedly took you some time to learn what was expected and how to get along in the new setting. You can expect that a child will have similar fears, problems, or hesitations. One of the first school-related behavior problems occurs when a five- or six-year-old refuses to go to school or wants to come home after he's gotten there. To a greater or lesser degree, not wanting to go to school is probably universal. Few of us can look back at our own childhoods without recalling at least some times when we developed mysterious (and rapidly passing) illnesses on school mornings, played hooky, or slipped away from school early. Somehow most of us survived a few such episodes without permanently and irreparably damaging our educational careers.

Difficulties occur, however, when children routinely start to balk at attending school. If children avoid going to school when they are very young, they may come to believe that school is optional and can be missed almost at will. For older children, there's another problem: not only will they fail to benefit from school activities on the days they miss, but they can rapidly slip behind in the work their classmates have covered. Catching up can be fairly difficult and unpleasant.

PREPARING YOUR CHILD TO BEGIN SCHOOL

When your five-year-old is about to start school, you can follow several steps to prepare for the forthcoming change in his or her life. The most important is conveying to your child that starting school is part of growing up and that school will be an enjoyable (and not a frightening) experience. Most kids have mixed feelings when it comes time to enter school. On one hand they know that going to school is expected of them, that it will make them feel more grown up, and that they will probably do things and meet friends they will like. Perhaps they have older brothers, sisters, or friends who have already begun school; joining these older people makes them feel, almost by association, more mature and higher in status. But at the same time leaving the security and familiarity of home can be a threatening experience for children, especially when it's for the first time.

Parents should begin to remind their children, well ahead of time, that school days are approaching. "Next year at this time you'll start school" or "At the end of the summer you'll be going to school with your sister" are effective reminders. As the time gets closer (say, a month before the school year begins), parents should have longer and more detailed talks with their child about school, describing (always at a level he can understand) the new and enjoyable things that will happen, how he will meet new friends and playmates, that he will now be more grown up, and most important, that you will feel proud to see him start school. You might mention some of the fond memories you have about what you did when you were in school. During the week before school will begin, plan to take a walk around the schoolyard with your child, have a picnic on the school grounds, and explore the school's interior with the youngster. In short, present school in a positive light so your child will look forward to the things that will happen there.

If your child is still anxious about starting school (or about leaving you), plan to accompany him or her to school on the first day or even the first few days. You may want to stay in the classroom for a short time in the morning, thereby reassuring the youngster that you want him to be there and that the schoolroom is a safe place to be. By all means let the teacher know that your youngster is a bit fearful of starting school; most teachers are used to this problem and will go out of their way to warmly reassure your child that school will be fun. You'll know that your child has adapted to starting school when he finds your presence in the classroom embarrassing and the extra reassurance from the teacher unnecessary, and when he would rather seek out friends or activities (instead of being near you) once he gets to the classroom.

There are times, however, when some kids simply decide that they don't want to go back to school at all.

WHEN CHILDREN SAY THEY WON'T GO TO SCHOOL

If your first-grade child gets up one morning and announces that he doesn't want to go to school, your first strategy is to ask why he doesn't feel like attending today. Much of the time, kids will say they'd rather be doing something else, don't like the work that will be covered that day, or just don't feel like going. All that's really needed is for you to acknowledge that all people sometimes feel like this, that the child will probably enjoy it once he gets to school, and that there will be time do do fun things at home after school is over. Then tell the child he will need to get ready to go.

The most common variation of the I-don't-want-to-go-to-school theme is the child's announcement that he is sick. Kids do this for two reasons. One is that they have learned that being sick is a socially acceptable excuse to stay home for the day. Also, not feeling well is the kind of thing that an outsider (even a parent) has trouble challenging because no one really knows how another person feels. Adults also use illness as a reason not to go to work when they'd rather be doing something else.

As a parent, your first responsibility is deciding whether your child is really ill, and if so, whether he is so sick that he can't go to school. To a certain degree you have to rely on your own judgment and intuition here. Be careful, though, not to let every report of a minor ache become a reason for staying home from school; that might encourage your child to complain and to become hypochondriacal. If you're not sure whether the child is very sick, schedule a trip to your doctor for the same day. That's the safest course for checking out any reported illness you think may be serious, and it also serves another purpose. One thing school-avoiding children tend to dislike even more than going to school is going to the doctor. If a child learns that being sick enough to miss school will probably mean a visit to the doctor the same day, he or she will be less likely to feign illness.

Another suggestion we make is that on days when the child misses school because he is sick, he should be treated as though he really is sick. Often when kids take a day off and aren't actually sick, they plan to spend the day doing things that are fun (like watching TV, playing games, or being outside). If your child does skip school and you're not certain he was sick enough to warrant it, make certain that he spends the day in bed, as if the illness were serious. When kids learn that school days missed will really be boring and spent in bed, they will find it more enjoyable and rewarding to go to school.

WHEN CHILDREN REFUSE TO GO TO SCHOOL

Trying to wheedle one's way out of going to school is a normal part of childhood and can be dealt with in the ways we've just discussed. Sometimes children will refuse to go to school more adamantly, by throwing tantrums and challenging their parents to make them go. This is potentially a more difficult problem, but it's one parents can learn to handle. First, has something happened at school that your child finds distressing or frightening? In most instances, kids who refuse to go to school simply don't enjoy school or like what they can do at home more than classroom activities. But at certain other times, children refuse to attend school because something genuinely frightening has happened to them there. In our clinic we occasionally see children who won't go to school because they have been bullied and intimidated by older children or have been ridiculed by a teacher when they performed badly on an assignment. Similarly, kids who lack sports skills may be genuinely fearful on gym class days. In these examples the problem is not so much that the child prefers to miss school as that the child is afraid to go to school.

If your child adamantly refuses to attend school, and especially if this is unusual for him or her, it is wise to investigate whether something frightening, embarrassing, or distressing has occurred recently. You can do this by quietly discussing how things have been at school and whether there is some reason why your child does not wish to attend class. Ask about specific things that could be upsetting to the youngster, such as whether there were any problems with classmates, the teacher, or schoolwork. Then call or visit the school to get similar information from the teacher. If your child has been refusing to go to school, the teacher should be made aware of that fact, as well as of your interest in resolving the problem. See whether the teacher has observed any difficulty your child has encountered, particularly anything that may have frightened or upset him.

If you are able to pinpoint a clearly upsetting incident, it will be important to spend some time discussing your child's fears or worries before you push the child back to school. In some cases your warm reassurance, encouragement, and support may be all that's needed, especially if the child's fears are minor. At other times a more specific plan of action may be needed to equip your child to handle the problem at school. While we cannot allow a child to miss school simply because the youngster encounters some difficulty there, it also isn't fair to expect him or her to want to attend without equipping the child to deal with real problems that are being encountered.

"Tomorrow, you'll be starting back to school." If your youngster has been missing school, he or she has already found out that it is possible to beat the going-to-school system; that's why the school-refusal problem exists. We want to change this

pattern around and put you back in control of your child's conduct. The best way to begin this is by sitting down with the child one evening and letting the youngster know that he will be returning to school the next day. How you tell this to your child is important. First, be certain in your own mind that you are entirely prepared to make your child go to school no matter what. If your child hasn't been attending, this simply means he's learned to outmaneuver your wishes that he go to school. You must now be extremely clear that missing school will stop and you should convey this the night before. Let the youngster know that regardless of what he does — whether he cries, tantrums, complains of a stomachache, refuses to get dressed — he will still be going to school tomorrow and every morning thereafter. This is a fact and it is unavoidable.

Getting ready for school in the morning. This is a critical point, since this is when the child will really have to get ready for school. In response to your firm talk on the previous night, the youngster may simply get ready and go with few problems. But more likely he will test your firmness, perhaps by crying, refusing to get out of bed or refusing to dress, complaining of illness, or by doing whatever else has worked in the past. No matter how difficult it is for you, your immediate task is to ignore any misbehaviors and calmly but very firmly stick with your plan to get the youngster to school. Most morning misbehaviors gradually stop once your child learns that they won't do any good and that going to school is the only acceptable course.

> *What if my child cries and tantrums?* Tell the youngster that tantrumming won't keep him from school, ask him to get ready, and then ignore further tantrumming. Be firm, but never let yourself get pulled into an angry yelling match.
>
> *What if he says he is ill but really isn't?* If the child is not really ill, tell the youngster that he'll feel better once he gets to school.

What if my child won't get dressed? Tell the child you will then take him to school in pajamas (with his clothes in a bag to change into there). If necessary, be prepared to do this.

What if he says he won't eat breakfast? Offer breakfast once and then let the youngster know he will miss it if he won't eat. If your child still won't have breakfast because he is angry about going to school, allow him to miss the meal that day.

What if my child just sits on the floor and screams? Again, calmly reiterate that he will go to school, tantrumming or not. Then, if need be, carry him to your car. Ignore the screaming.

The point of all this is that even if your child objects to going to school, you must be willing to firmly and unemotionally follow through, even if it involves carrying him to your car for the ride to school. Once you've picked the day your child will return to class, don't back down from that decision. It will only make the problem tougher to solve later on.

These steps often sound quite coercive and dictatorial to parents. As we noted earlier, the best way to promote your child's good behavior is by reinforcing it positively, but before we can reward the good behavior of going to school, we first have to get the child there. Pleading, discussing, begging, or threatening are all ineffective and may even make the problem worse. A far better approach — for your child's sake — consists of taking the calm but firm position that the child will attend school (even if the child misbehaves to avoid it) and then making sure the youngster gets there, even if it involves literally carrying the youngster (kicking, yelling, and tantrumming) through the school's front door in his pajamas. As soon as the child finds that you'll really do this, the problem is well on the way to being solved.

While your child is at school . . . If a youngster throws

tantrums at home to avoid going to school and is still doing this on the way through the school door when you drop him off, won't the child be a terrible behavior problem once he is in the classroom? In a surprising number of cases, the answer is no. Quite often, once a first-grade child is back at school, he settles into the classroom routine quite well. This usually happens when the child accepts the fact that he will be there because his parents simply won't allow any more stay-at-home days. Also, some youngsters who tantrum and behave childishly with their parents will stop doing so when other kids are around because crying about school when you're there isn't likely to gain much sympathy from the other kids in the class.

Plan several other steps to help your child settle into the school routine:

1. Before your child returns to school, let the teacher know he or she will be coming back. Ask the teacher to make it a point to welcome the child, praise him for returning to school, and provide some extra positive attention, especially during the first few days back. This will serve to reinforce school attendance. Teachers are almost always willing to take such extra steps to help solve this kind of behavior problem.

2. In the same conversation, alert the teacher to the possibility that your child might look for reasons to leave school, especially during the first few days back. In the vast majority of cases, the child says he is ill and asks to go home. Explain to the teacher that it is your wish that the child stay at school unless a genuine emergency is at hand, and suggest that the teacher try to ignore any attempts by the child to manipulate his way home for the day. The only exception to this should be if the child is really sick enough to merit a trip to the doctor.

3. When your child returns home after the first day back at school, strongly praise the child for attending. Do this even if it was extremely difficult to get the child to school

that morning. Congratulate the youngster for going to school "like a big boy [or girl]" and tell him you are proud of his conduct. Arrange for some special reward or special activity after school that will further reinforce the child's improved conduct. Finally, attentively discuss with your youngster the good things that happened at school that day, including the fun things he did, friends he saw, work he accomplished, and so on. Try to focus the discussion on positive events rather than on problems that may perpetuate a negative attitude toward school. As your child learns to talk about enjoyable school activities, he will start to think of school itself as more enjoyable.

4. Be prepared for the possibility that it might take a number of days for your child to go to school willingly. Every morning, handle getting ready for school the same way you did the first morning. If your child objects to getting ready, tantrums, or feigns illness, be firm and steadfast, just as you were the first morning. As soon as you observe the child behaving even a little bit better in the morning, let him know that you've noticed the improvement and appreciate it.

5. By following all of these steps, most parents can successfully get their children back to school. Occasionally, though, problems may develop that parents or teachers cannot handle on their own. These usually involve more serious separation fears or classroom behavior problems that continue even after the child has arrived at school. Professional consultation is in order if these difficulties persist for more than one week after a parent has taken the steps we describe here.

HELPING YOUR CHILD MAKE FRIENDS AND OVERCOME SHYNESS

So far we have discussed the transition points as a child starts attending day-care or begins going to school for the first time.

One reason these are transition points is because the youngster is now physically separated from his family for part of each day. But along with this physical distancing from home, your child is also entering new and expanded social environments. The earliest parts of a child's life are largely spent with the immediate family and people close to the family. As children get older, more and more of their time is spent with new people: playmates who live in the neighborhood, other kids who go to the same preschool or elementary school, and other adults such as teachers. By the time a child is five or six, the skill of playing cooperatively with others is an important part of the youngster's life. Interestingly, while younger children do play together, their interactions often involve playing near others but without a great deal of mutual exchange and conversation. By around five years, social activities start becoming more elaborate, reciprocal, and conversational in nature.

We mentioned earlier that complete fearlessness is not an ideal characteristic in children. Similarly, we should also keep in mind that there is nothing at all wrong with a child who happens to be a bit shy. In fact, it can be harmful for a parent to impose the expectation that a child be outgoing, extraverted, and the center of attention if the youngster's basic interpersonal style is more quiet and reflective. It is best to consider a child's shyness a problem if it is so extreme that the youngster is unable to make or keep friends, won't (or can't) seek out the company of age-mates, and feels unhappy as a result of these inabilities.

Extreme shyness in childhood can cause difficulties for several reasons, being that overly shy children don't get as much enjoyment and gratification from social situations as they should. The girl who always plays alone during school recess, the boy who watches TV inside all day because he can't make friends with others his own age, and the youngster who is always left out of games with other children all miss important opportunities to have fun with others. Shyness also operates as a vicious cycle. If a young child is very shy and lacks the skills needed to get along with others, he will be somewhat isolated from them. Because he spends little time with peers, the youngster will have fewer everyday opportunities to learn, see, and practice the very friend-making skills that could help overcome the initial shyness problem. As a result, shy young children may become shy older children, shy older children may become shy adolescents, and shy adolescents may become shy adults.

Happily, this pattern can be changed. Sometimes change happens on its own, without any special planning. For example, a shy only child who lacks neighborhood playmates may, when starting school, overcome this initial shyness simply because there suddenly are more children his age around. The quiet child (or, for that matter, the quiet adult) can start to bloom socially when he or she happens to meet a few other friendly people who share similar interests and personality styles. Parents are in a position to help children overcome problems of excessive shyness in two ways: first, by creating more opportunities for the child to make friends and to interact with them; second, by actually teaching the youngster some of the skills needed to get along with others in those situations.

CREATING OPPORTUNITIES FOR YOUR CHILD
TO MAKE FRIENDS

To be able to make friends, one has to spend time with other people who might become friends; it is certain that a child can't make friends if his time is typically spent alone or only with parents. As a first step, we want to arrange for a youngster to have plenty of opportunities to meet others of approximately his own age. Here are some ways to do this:

1. If there is a preschool program in your neighborhood, consider enrolling your child in it on a part-time basis. If your youngster has not yet reached school age, spending several hours a day in a setting with other children provides opportunities to meet others and learn cooperative and friend-making skills. If your child is extremely shy, begin this process slowly, with the youngster spending only a few hours a week at the center. As the child becomes more comfortable with others, you can gradually increase his time there. In addition to the general features of good preschool programs we discussed earlier, look for a very active program that stresses group games and cooperative projects among the children, a program with a dedicated staff that will make certain a shy youngster is brought into the group. At least initially, you may want to spend some time with your child at the center to help him get used to it.

2. *Explore church school programs and social activities for children of your child's age.* Above and beyond weekly Sunday school classes, many churches have other social and activity programs for children of all ages, including preschoolers. If your child is shy and needs to spend more time with others, look into these programs. They are generally well supervised, usually by adults who like children and who share values similar to your own.

3. *For children who are at or near school age, the local YMCA/YWCA, Boys' Club, Parents Without Partners, or similar groups often offer youth programs.* While some of these are supervised craft, recreational, and hobby programs for groups of children, other programs are planned to allow parents and their children to participate together. One typical program, offered by the YMCA for many years, is called Indian Guides and involves regular meetings, games, and even camping trips for groups of fathers and their sons. A similar program is operated by the YWCA for girls and their mothers. These kinds of programs are excellent, combining opportunities for very shy children to meet others in a nonthreatening environment and with the parent reassuringly nearby. Again, check with your local "Y" or similar organizations to learn of available social activities for boys and girls. Planned outings

to the zoo, to a beach, or on a picnic with the families of your acquaintances also allow children to meet other youngsters in a natural and comfortable way.

HELPING YOUR CHILD LEARN TO MAKE FRIENDS

Being physically near others, whether at preschool or in the backyard, doesn't necessarily mean a child is actively interacting with them. At almost every playground we can find some children who remain at the outskirts of what is taking place, watching but not joining in the activities of others. This is part of childhood shyness and often means that the youngster doesn't yet know how to go about joining in others' games, playing or talking with them, and so on. Until the child learns friend-making skills, he or she will have difficulty overcoming shyness.

You can assume some of the responsibility for teaching your child how to make friends and play well with others. There are four basic parts to this skills-teaching process: (1) instruction, (2) modeling or showing your child how to behave, (3) arranging for your child to practice making friends, and (4) praising or reinforcing the child's efforts to become less shy. In general, these approaches work best for children five years and older.

Instruction. If you feel your child is extremely shy, it is probably because you have noticed that the youngster doesn't play well with other children and doesn't do some of those things that are needed to effectively meet, join, and play with friends. Consider James, a six-year-old who came to the clinic because his parents felt he couldn't make friends. In order to see exactly how James acted with others, we visited his school and actually watched how he behaved with his first-grade classmates at recess, playtime, and during activities when the children could mingle informally. We noticed that James played alone, away from others, that he rarely greeted classmates or talked with them, and that he seemed unable to join in his classmates' games. Based on what we saw, we agreed with the parents that James was a very shy child, primarily because he didn't do those things that are needed to establish friendships. It was our feeling that he didn't yet know *how* to make friends.

To overcome this problem, a first step is to teach the youngster what he can do to get along better with others. In James' case we provided instructions for him: certain friend-making hints or rules were explained just before he went to school or before he went outside to join a group of neighborhood children:

"Say hi if you want to make a friend!"

"If someone is playing, ask if you can too!"

"Say hello to people by using their names—Hi Joe! Hi Susan! Hi James!"

"If you're playing and somebody comes up, ask them to play with you, too!"

Keep in mind that because children, especially young ones, cannot remember complicated instructions, it's best to rehearse only one or two friend-making skills immediately before the child has an opportunity to try them out. Pick those skills with which your youngster seems to have trouble at present and gently remind the child to use them whenever he wants to play with others. Your aim isn't to nag or to make your child feel self-conscious; it's to provide him with some practical hints.

Model and practice friend-making skills with your child. As we pointed out in chapter 4, it is usually easier to show how to do something than to tell about it. For this reason we often advise parents to actually model or demonstrate for the child how to go about making friends. In our clinic sessions and during at-home visits with James and his parents, skills for making friends were modeled. As part of a Friend-Making Game James was asked to pretend that he was really at school, perhaps working on an art project or standing on the playground. Then we asked him to make believe that his parent was really another child who wanted to play with him. The parent would then model how to start playing:

Parent as model: "Hi James! What are you doing?"
James: "Nothing much."
Parent as model: "Do you want to play with the cars?"
James: "Okay."
Parent as model: "Good. Let's go play with them. I'd like to do that."

As the parent and child were play-acting this everyday interaction, James had the chance to see and hear exactly what another child would do in the role-played situation (that's why this is a form of teaching). The situations modeled in these nightly practices were based on encounters that James might actually have at school or in the neighborhood and gave him a start in learning how to walk up and start a conversation, how to ask to join in the games of others, how to ask others to play with him, and so on.

Each exercise then shifted its focus so that James could practice what his parent had just modeled. Now James played himself and the parent became a child James wanted to meet. James practiced what he would say in that situation: "Hi Tom! What are you doing? Do you want to play cars?" and so on, with the parent acting the way Tom might when James approached him.

Here are some useful steps to follow for this kind of practice:

1. Plan to use a short Friend-Making Game like the one we've just described. Your modeling/practice sessions should be short (no more than ten minutes), but plan to have them often, perhaps after dinner each evening.
2. Pick only one situation to rehearse in each session, se-

lecting the kinds of encounters in which your child is now extremely shy. If you one day saw your youngster look as if really wanted to join a group of kids next door (but he didn't), you might want to practice how to handle this situation during your Friend-Making Game for the next few nights.

3. The essential ingredients in this approach consist of giving instructions to your child concerning how to handle the situation you are role-playing; then modeling so your child can see and hear how someone would act in that situation; and allowing the child to rehearse or practice the skill with you. Don't let these sessions become nag times in which you keep telling your youngster how to act toward peers. What makes the approach effective (and fun) is that it allows your child to watch what you would do and then actively practice the same thing himself.

4. The tone of the practice sessions is also critical. Think of them as a way to directly help your child learn to handle some currently difficult situations better, not as a way to make the youngster develop a new personality. The sessions should be introduced to your child as a game, upbeat and positive in tone. Make frequent use of praise, especially at the important point where the child role-plays his responses after he has watched you model them. If you don't use enough praise to reinforce the youngster's new skill development, the approach will be ineffective and your child will dislike the Friend-Making Game.

5. Some variations can be made in handling these sessions. James, for example, liked puppets, so we used puppets to model and practice friend-making skills in some of our sessions. James, with a hand puppet, would pretend that figure was himself and would speak for it. My puppet would be named for another child actually in his first-grade class, and I would speak for it. My puppet modeled how to handle situations that might really occur at school, and after this modeling James would have his

puppet use the same skills while play-acting with mine. The idea and the principles are the same as those we've discussed, but we used puppets because James found this more interesting than always role-playing face to face. You too can vary the basic skills-teaching procedure by using puppets, dolls, or similar things to keep up your child's interest.

6. Keep in mind that while we call this the Friend-Making Game, it isn't merely a play activity. Its purpose is to improve your child's interpersonal skills and help him overcome shyness. For it to work, the youngster must start to use these skills with other children. Before your child goes off to preschool, elementary school, or outside to play, remind him to "do the same things as when we play the Friend-Making Game" and mention what they are (walking up to others, greeting them by name, asking to play and joining, and so on). This will help make the connection between the practice game and those real-life situations in which the youngster has been very shy. Be careful not to make your child feel self-conscious; a brief reminder is sufficient.

7. Finally, keep alert to any occasions in which your child does try to use the skills you've worked on. If one day you notice from the kitchen window that your youngster walks up to a group of children and starts talking, and if this had been difficult for him in the past, let the child know later that you observed this change and were pleased to see it. Similarly, praise any other signs that the child is becoming less shy. These signs might include your child's reports that he played or talked to others, occasions when the child visits friends' houses or has friends come over, and any other peer interactions that you see take place.

As we mentioned, all children have different personalities and social styles. Some are naturally quiet and reflective, while others are naturally outgoing. This is part of life's diversity and should certainly not be a cause for concern. On the other hand, if a child is so painfully shy that he or she can't meet others, can't play with them or make friends, the problem merits the parent's attention. The approaches we've discussed here can solve some of these problems. If, however, longer-range patterns of friendlessness and extreme shyness develop, a professional can offer additional suggestions and guidance.

10/
When Outside
Help Is Needed

THE first youngster to make it all the way through childhood
without any problems has probably not yet been born. As we
pointed out early in this book, at some time or another all
kids exhibit misbehaviors that frustrate and concern their
parents, or fail to behave well at certain times, or have trouble
learning some of the self-control skills that need to be mastered
in early life. The nature of childhood — with its many new
tasks and challenges — and the nature of children — who have
had very little experience in the process of living — virtually
ensure that behavior problems will occasionally develop.

As we have also seen, the most common behavior problems
of children can be overcome when a parent learns how to
handle the child's misbehavior differently. In our clinic, we
find that children with troublesome and sometimes longstanding problems like temper tantrums, noncompliance, bed-
wetting, and childhood fears respond well — and often quite
quickly — to the techniques we have described in previous
chapters.

When parents understand how to arrange consequences that
will foster their child's good behavior skills and will discourage
continued behavior problems, and when they actually put these
principles into effect, many common misbehavior patterns can
be solved without outside help. Nevertheless, there are certain
times when parents and children can benefit from individual-
ized, professional consultation to help solve a youngster's be-

havior problems. For example, you should consider seeking outside assistance if:

- you've consistently been handling your youngster's behavior problems in the ways we have outlined but you have not seen much improvement, usually by a month for most of the problems discussed in this book;
- your child doesn't seem to respond to techniques like time-out or positive attention to reinforce his good behavior, even when used in the way we've described, and you feel some extra tailoring of the approaches is needed;
- your child seems depressed and unhappy, or is doing things that might result in harm to himself;
- you have questions about your child's emotional or educational development and would simply like to discuss them with a professional.

Seeking expert advice is important at times like these. Unfortunately, though, many parents don't have access to the information that can guide them in locating a professional who can provide good, practical advice about children's behavior problems. There has probably been far more written about how to find a plumber or an electrician than about finding someone who can advise parents on children's behavior problems. If you decide to consult an expert, what kind of professional should it be, how do you locate someone who will be very good, and what exactly should you expect from the individual you are consulting?

Some people claim to be experts on children's behavior problems but may provide information that doesn't help or may even harm your child. In our own clinic we have seen children who for months received daily "motivational spankings" because the parents were advised by a teacher that severe punishment is the best way to encourage a child to do homework. Other youngsters who came to us with ordinary behavior problems had been misdiagnosed as emotionally disturbed and placed on large doses of medication that only made them sleepy and dull. And children with problems like bed-wetting which can devastate a youngster's self-esteem, were allowed to continue experiencing this difficulty for years because a parent was told that youngsters eventually outgrow it or, worse yet, was informed that bed-wetting cannot be treated. Locating effective outside help for a child's behavior problems is something you may never need to do, but a wise parent will want to know how to find a good professional if this expertise is ever needed.

Several kinds of mental health practitioners can provide advice to parents about their children. These include psychologists, clinical social workers, family counselors, and psychiatrists. Just as there are various kinds of specialists, professionals use different approaches for treating the problems of children. The approach of a specific therapist is usually determined by that professional's own understanding of the causes of children's difficulties and the most effective ways to treat them. While there are many different methods for treating a child's difficulties, the approach we have used throughout this book is based on the principle of *behavior therapy*. This system for solving problems is relatively new in the field of psychology; most of its techniques have been developed and refined over the past twenty years. Several characteristics of behavior therapy set it apart from other ways of handling the problems of children:

Behavior therapy focuses on the actual problems your child is having and attempts to change them directly. Rather than exploring for the hidden past causes of problems, which may have little bearing on what is needed to solve them, behavior therapy is straightforward and focuses on solving problems directly rather than merely describing their causes.

Behavior therapy uses principles that help your child actively learn to overcome problems. Psychologists who study how people learn from their experience — as behavior therapists do — are able to apply those principles to the problems of children. For example, overcoming fear through progressive but gradual exposure to what you are afraid of, strengthening good behavior patterns through praise and attention, and denying attention when a child misbehaves are all approaches that help a child change and learn from experience.

Behavior therapy is a skills-training approach for parents because the therapist provides parents with specific advice on how to handle a child's behavior problems.

Behavior therapy is a skill-training approach for children, because as the parent learns to handle the child differently when he misbehaves or experiences difficulties, the youngster will have the opportunity to exercise more responsible, positive, and self-controlled patterns of behavior.

Behavior therapy approaches are neither extremely punitive nor extremely permissive. Instead, as we have stressed repeatedly, this approach helps children learn to behave well through understanding of the consequences of their actions, teaches skills that will help a youngster feel more self-confident and successful, and guides a child in learning right from wrong based on his experiences rather than from schooling, lecturing, or spanking.

As we pointed out, behavior therapy is certainly not the only way to treat children's difficulties; other approaches can also be effective. But if you decide to seek a behavioral form of professional consultation, here are several steps you can follow.

HOW TO FIND A BEHAVIOR THERAPY SPECIALIST FOR CHILDREN

Social workers, family counselors, and psychiatrists may use behavior therapy techniques, but the professionals most likely to follow this approach are psychologists. Many of the guidelines described here, however, apply to other kinds of professionals as well. Psychologists are individuals who, in most states, must have a doctoral degree in psychology (Ph.D. or

Psy.D.) and must be licensed to practice in this field. Clinical psychologists who have had specialized training in the development and problems of children are the professionals frequently consulted by parents concerned about their children's difficulties. They usually have at least four years of graduate school and one year of internship training before they become eligible to practice.

How does a parent find a psychologist? The very best way is by referral from someone you know whose judgment you can trust. If you have a friend, relative, or neighbor who has seen a psychologist (or, even better, whose child has been treated by a psychologist), ask for that person's experiences and recommendation. If a friend or relative has had a positive experience with a child psychologist, the individual will probably be happy to share a recommendation with you. Even if you find that the professional doesn't treat children, good adult psychologists can often direct you to good child psychologists. Don't be shy about asking people you know well for their advice. Another way to find a psychologist is by asking your pediatrician or family doctor. While psychologists themselves aren't physicians, most family doctors know the psychologists in your community and can refer you to one who specializes in behavior therapy.

Finally, certain agencies and organizations can provide parents with the names of local child psychologists. A parent might call the psychology training program at a major university for the names of practicing psychologists in the area or a community mental health center. One national organization, the Association for the Advancement of Behavior Therapy (420 Lexington Avenue, New York, NY 10170), provides information about psychologists, social workers, and psychiatrists who use this approach in most major cities. Keep in mind that while organizations (whether universities, mental health centers, or professional associations) can provide the names of psychologists, they usually aren't able to tell you who will be best for your child, who is most experienced and skilled, or who you will like. That's the reason referrals and recommendations made by satisfied clients or other people whose judgment you know you can trust are the best ways to find a psychologist.

Once you have found a psychologist, the next step is to arrange an initial consultation visit to discuss your child's behavior problems. Parents should regard any first visit to a psychologist as a preliminary session, one that allows them to explain the youngster's difficulties and also allows them to learn about the specialist's approach. An initial session of this kind should not be seen as an immediate commitment to longer-range therapy but as an opportunity to share information with the professional. From that discussion a decision can be made concerning further sessions.

What should a parent discuss (and look for) during a preliminary consultation session with a child psychologist? Clearly, not all psychologists (even those who share a behavioral approach to treatment) handle initial sessions in the same way, but certain matters should be raised in any first visit.

Ask about the psychologist's training, especially with children. While you shouldn't challenge or grill the individual to prove his or her qualifications to you, it is appropriate to inquire where the individual received training, what degree the professional has earned, and what the individual's child treatment background is. If you are consulting a psychologist who practices independently, the person should have a Ph.D. in clinical psychology and should be licensed in your state. If the individual has less than this amount of training or is still in training (as is true in some clinics or mental health centers), the therapist's immediate supervisor should have these credentials. Inquire about his or her specific background in child treatment. This specialization is more difficult for a parent to evaluate, since good child psychologists can gain their expertise in graduate training, during their internships, as part of their later practice experience, or in some combination of these three ways. However, expect to find evidence that the person has had substantial background treating children's problems, even if the psychologist's practice is not limited to children.

Does the psychologist practice behavior therapy? The approach to children's problems we have followed in this book is based on behavior therapy principles. The best way to find out whether that is also the psychologist's approach is simply by asking.

After explaining in detail your youngster's current difficulties and answering questions asked by the psychologist, ask for his thoughts on the problem's cause and treatment. No therapist can ever completely understand your child's difficulties in a single consultation; in fact, it may take several visits and a good deal of questioning before the psychologist can propose a strategy for solving the child's difficulty. However, the individual should at least be able to outline some preliminary thoughts about the causes of your youngster's behavior problems and what can be done to help the child overcome those problems. Look particularly for indications that the psychologist will be prepared to give you detailed, practical, and specific advice on how to handle your child's behavior problems, or that he or she will focus on teaching your child skills the youngster now lacks.

Use your own intuitive judgment as to whether the professional's initial formulation of your child's difficulty makes sense and seems practical. For example, if the youngster has a bed-wetting problem that proved difficult for you to handle on your own, it is logical to assume that the therapist will question you about details of the problem (when it occurs, how often the child bed-wets, whether you've had a medical checkup for the child, what you've done to handle it, how your child feels after a wetting episode, and so on). The psychologist may ask you to keep notes or records of how often the child bed-wets. Most important, the treatment proposed should be one that seems directly aimed at the problem you are having. When parents consult a psychologist about a specific problem they should get practical, useful, direct information on how to solve that problem.

How long does treatment usually last for this type of problem? Behavior therapy consultation tailors specific treatments to specific problems the child has in a precise and focused approach. While no professional can predict the exact number of consultation sessions a given problem will require, experienced psychologists should be able to give you a general idea of how long the treatment usually takes. If your therapist predicts an extended course of visits for a problem that seems fairly straightforward, you may wish to consult another person for a second opinion.

It is also wise for parents to keep an eye on whether progress is being made once the family begins consulting a professional. In our clinic, we usually advise parents that for most problems some change in the child's behavior should be evident within three to five visits if the parent diligently follows the recommendations we make. This doesn't mean that difficult problems can be resolved in this period of time; it does, however, mean that some improvement should be evident before too many consultation sessions pass by. Many psychologists actually set a point (such as after five sessions) at which the parent and the professional will get together to review the progress made.

Be very cautious if medication is suggested for routine problems before other approaches are tried. Psychologists never prescribe medication because they aren't physicians. But parents sometimes do see medical doctors who suggest the long-term use of tranquilizers, stimulants, and similar medications to change a child's behavior. When parents are concerned and frustrated by their children's conduct and when they realize something is wrong with the youngster's behavior, the idea of giving medicine to cure the problem has a certain amount of appeal. Although there are some distinct childhood disorders for which medication is needed, these are usually neurological (brain function) disorders which may also affect the child's behavior. For example, children with seizures or epilepsy often need medication to prevent them from having seizures. Some children suffer from a severe and unusual disorder called autism that results in extreme withdrawal from others, little or no speech development, preoccupation with inanimate objects, and self-injurious behavior (such as repeated self-biting). Autistic children also appear to have a neurological disease that requires medication. But these fairly rare disorders are very different from the behavior problems, insecurities or fears, and self-control problems that lead many parents to seek outside help.

Unfortunately, too many physicians rely primarily on medication to treat problems that don't require it. Children with temper and anger problems are often given tranquilizers rather than being taught how to control anger on their own. Kids who seem unhappy and listless are given antidepressant medications rather than being encouraged to find activities that will allow them to be happier. And, most common of all, some children who are simply active and poorly behaved are too quickly called hyperactive and placed on stimulant medication. Often, what is really needed is more consistent, effective parenting and discipline.

What should a parent do if told that his or her child should be given medication to control everyday behavior problems? Any decision concerning medication for a child's behavior problems must take into account the short- and long-range effects of the medication. For example, many parents don't know that certain drugs given to hyperactive children can affect the youngster's growth or disrupt his sleeping and eating patterns. It is especially tragic when children early in life become dependent on medications and learn to attribute their behavior to drugs rather than to their own ability to overcome problems.

As a parent, keep in mind that professional opinions vary widely on whether children should be given medication for behavior problems. Also, remember that different approaches can be used to solve the same problem. So if one professional immediately suggests medication for your child's behavior problem, it is generally wise to seek other professionals' opinions. A less extreme approach may be just as effective.

If I seek professional advice for my child's difficulty, won't the behavior therapist spend most of his or her time with my youngster? Parents are sometimes surprised to find that a psychologist may spend more time talking with them than with the child. A major reason for this is that because the child's difficulties probably occur at home or when the child is with his family, it is important that the parents learn how to handle the youngster when and where his problems actually occur. A good deal of time may need to be spent on providing suggestions to the parents. In a sense, a good therapist serves as a consultant to parents, advising them how to help their child through difficulties the youngster is having. So while a psychologist will always want to spend time with your child, he may spend as much or even more time with you.

Is it best to consult a behavioral psychologist of the same sex as my child? Although there aren't many studies on this, it probably doesn't matter, especially for children. Parents should select a psychologist they like and feel is competent regardless of whether the specialist is a man or a woman.

All of these suggestions are intended to help you if you decide you want to consult a professional about your child. Keep in mind, however, that behavior problems of the kind we have discussed in this book are encountered by virtually all children. Because childhood is a time of new experiences, challenges, and growth, it is also a time when problems will occasionally develop and require solution. For you, the parent, this book has presented some approaches for solving the common difficulties most parents face with their three- to six-year-olds. For your child, we hope the suggestions made here will help in the process of outgrowing problems, achieving successes, and feeling confident.

Appendix

Some Common Problems That Parents Encounter with Their Children

Age of Child	Problems or Tasks Common at This Age	Comments
Three to four	Fear of the dark and fear of sleeping alone	Fears or insecurities about being away from one's parents (especially at night and in the dark) are quite common among children three to four (see chapter 7).
Three to five	Consistent toilet use	Most children are toilet trained earlier than three, but some youngsters still encounter toilet use problems for years after the first attempts at training (see chapter 6).
Three to five	Starting day-care	Starting day-care itself isn't a problem, but steps should be taken to select a good center and to prepare your child for it if he will begin day-care during this age period (see chapter 9).
Three to six	Bed-wetting	Nighttime bed-wetting often occurs even after daytime toilet use is successful. If frequent bed-wetting is a problem past the age of three, a parent should work to solve it (see chapter 6).
Three to six	Noncompliance	Noncompliance can be a problem at any age, but often becomes more difficult as children get older (see chapter 5).
Four to six	Tantrums	During infancy, crying is one of the few ways children can

Age of Child	Problems or Tasks Common at This Age	Comments
		use to communicate hurt, fear, or discomfort to others. As children get older, tantrums become more purposeful (usually to try to get something or when the child feels frustrated). Our aim is to reduce tantrums and to help the child develop more acceptable ways to communicate displeasure verbally (see chapter 5).
Four to six	Fears of objects, situations, or things	As children reach this age, fears become more focused and specific. Some common ones are fear of animals, doctors, and the hospital (see chapter 7).
Four to six	Decision-making	Even in childhood, learning to make decisions ("What crayon color should this be?" "Should I go outside?" "What's there to do?") helps youngsters become able to think for themselves (see chapter 8).
Four to six	Making friends	Social skills become important as children spend more of their time with others and begin school (see chapter 9).
Five to six	Dawdling	Dawdling can be a problem when children become old enough to take some responsibility for getting ready for school, day-care, or bed (see chapter 6).
Five to six	Starting school	Especially for youngsters who have not been in day-care, beginning school represents a major change in the routine. Helping the child prepare for it is important (see chapter 9).

References

Most of the approaches to solving children's behavior problems described in this book are based on techniques derived from the child psychology and child behavior therapy literature. Presented below are some of the studies that form the basis for many of the approaches we have discussed.

CHAPTER 2

Ayllon, T., Layman, D., and Kandel, H. J. "A behavioral-educational alternative to drug control of hyperactive children." *Journal of Applied Behavior Analysis* 8 (1975):421–433.

Harris, F. R., Johnston, M. K., Kelley, C. S., and Wolf, M. M. "Effects of positive social reinforcement on regressed crawling of a nursery school child." *Journal of Educational Psychology* 20 (1964):8–17.

Herbert, E. W. and Baer, D. M. "Training parents as behavior modifiers: Self-recording of contingent attention." *Journal of Applied Behavior Analysis* 5 (1972):139–149.

Homme, L. E., DeBaca, P. C., Devine, J. V., Stunhorst, R., and Rickert, E. J. "Use of the Premack principle in controlling the behavior of nursery school children." *Journal of the Experimental Analysis of Behavior* 6 (1963):544.

Johnson, C. A. and Katz, R. C. "Using parents as change agents for their children: A review." *Journal of Child Psychology and Psychiatry and Allied Disciplines* 14 (1973):181–200.

Risley, T. "Learning and lollipops." *Psychology Today* 1 (1968):28–31, 62–65.

CHAPTER 3

Allen, K. E., Henke, L. B., Harris, F. R., Baer, D. M., and Reynolds, N. J. "Control of hyperactivity by social reinforcement of attending behavior." *Journal of Educational Psychology* 58 (1967):231–237.

Baer, D. M. "Laboratory control of thumbsucking by withdrawal and reinstatement of reinforcement." *Journal of Experimental Analysis of Behavior* 5 (1962):525–528.

Bandura, A. *Aggression: A social learning analysis.* Englewood Cliffs, N.J.: Prentice-Hall, 1973.

Benoit, R. B. and Mayer, G. R. "Timeout: Guidelines for its selection and use." *The Personnel and Guidance Journal* 53 (1975):501–506.

Goetz, E. M., Holmberg, M. C., and LeBlanc, J. M. "Differential reinforcement of other behavior and noncontingent reinforcement as control procedures during the modification of a preschooler's compliance." *Journal of Applied Behavior Analysis* 8 (1975):77–82.

Harris, V. W. and Sherman, J. A. "Use and analysis of the 'Good Behavior Game' to reduce disruptive classroom behavior." *Journal of Applied Behavior Analysis* 6 (1973):405–417.

Wolf, M. M., Risley, T. R., and Mees, H. "Application of operant conditioning procedures to the behavior problems of an autistic child." *Behavior Research and Therapy* 1 (1964):303–312.

CHAPTER 4

Bandura, A., Ross, D., and Ross, S. A. "Imitation of film-mediated aggressive models." *Journal of Abnormal Social Psychology* 66 (1963):3–11.

Bandura, A. and McDonald, F. J. "The influence of social reinforcement and the behavior of models in shaping children's moral judgments." *Journal of Abnormal Social Psychology* 67 (1963):274–281.

Bandura, A. and Walters, R. H. *Social learning and personality development.* New York: Holt, Rinehart and Winston, 1963.

Geller, M. I. and Scheirer, C. J. "The effect of film modeling on cooperative play in disadvantaged preschoolers." *Journal of Abnormal Child Psychology* 6 (1978):71–87.

Kuhn, D. Z., Madsen, C. H., and Becker, W. C. "Effects of exposure to an aggressive model and 'frustration' on children's aggressive behavior." *Child Development* 38 (1967):739–745.

Thomas, M. H. and Drabman, R. S. "Tolerance of real life aggression as a function of exposure to televised violence and age of child." *Merrill-Palmer Quarterly* 21 (1975):227–232.

CHAPTER 5

Bornstein, M., Bellack, A. S., and Hersen, M. "Social skills training for highly aggressive children." *Behavior Modification* 4 (1980):173–186.

Brown, P and Elliott, R. "Control of aggression in a nursery school class." *Journal of Experimental Child Psychology* 2 (1965):103–107.

Williams, C. "The elimination of tantrum behavior by extinction procedures." *Journal of Abnormal Child Psychology* 59 (1959):269.

Zielberger, J., Sampen, S. E., and Sloane, H. N. "Modification of a child's problem behaviors in the home with the mother as a therapist." *Journal of Applied Behavior Analysis* 1 (1968):47–54.

CHAPTER 6

Azrin, N. H. and Foxx, R. M. *Toilet training in less than a day*. New York: Simon & Schuster, 1974.

Collins, R. W. "Importance of bladder-cue buzzer contingency in the conditioning treatment for enuresis." *Journal of Abnormal Psychology* 82 (1973):299–308.

Drabman, R. S., Spitalnik, R., and O'Leary, K. D. "Teaching self-control to disruptive children." *Journal of Abnormal Psychology* 82 (1973):10–16.

Drabman, R. S. and Creedon, D. L. "Beat the buzzer." *Child Behavior Therapy* 1 (1979):295–296.

Foxx, R. M. and Azrin, N. H. "Dry pants: A rapid method of toilet training children." *Behavior Research and Therapy* 11 (1973):435–442.

Matson, J. L. and Ollendick, T. H. "Issues in toilet training normal children." *Behavior Therapy* 8 (1977):549–553.

CHAPTER 7

Giebenharn, J. E. and O'Dell, S. L. "Evaluation of a parent training manual for reducing children's fear of the dark." *Journal of Applied Behavior Analysis* (in press).

Graziano, A. M., DeGiovianni, I. S., and Garcia, K. A. "Behavioral treatment of children's fears: A review." *Psychological Bulletin* 86 (1979):804–830.

Leitenberg, H. and Callahan, E. J. "Reinforced practice and reduction of different kinds of fears in adults and children." *Behavior Research and Therapy* 11 (1973):19–30.

Melamed, B. G., Hawes, R. R., Heiby, E., and Gluck, J. "The use of filmed modeling to reduce uncooperative behavior of children during dental treatment." *Journal of Dental Research* 51 (1975):797–801.

Melamed, B. G. and Siegel, L. "Reduction of anxiety in children facing hospitalization and surgery by use of filmed modeling." *Journal of Consulting and Clinical Psychology* 43 (1975):511–521.

CHAPTER 8

Adler, A. *What life should mean to you.* Boston: Little, Brown, 1931.

Bem, S. L. "The measurement of psychological androgyny." *Journal of Consulting and Clinical Psychology* 42 (1974):155–162.

Chittenden, G. E. "An experimental study in measuring and modifying assertive behavior in young children." *Monographs of the Society for Research in Child Development* 7 (1942) (1, serial no. 31).

Kelly, J. A. and Worell, L. "Parent behaviors related to masculine, feminine and androgynous sex role orientations." *Journal of Consulting Psychology* 44 (1976):843–851.

Spivak, G. and Shure, M. B. *Social adjustment of young children: A cognitive approach to solving real life problems.* San Francisco: Jossey-Bass, 1974.

CHAPTER 9

Belsky, J. and Steinberg, L. D. "The effects of daycare: A critical review." *Child Development* 49 (1978):929–949.

Evers, W. and Schwartz, J. "Modifying social withdrawal in preschoolers: The effects of filmed modeling and teacher praise." *Journal of Abnormal Child Psychology* 1 (1973):248–256.

Gottman, J., Gonso, J., and Rasmussen, B. "Social interaction, social competence and friendship in children." *Child Development* 46 (1975):708–718.

Gottman, J., Gonso, J., and Schuler, P. "Teaching social skills to isolated children." *Child Development* 47 (1976):179–197.

Kelly, J. A. "Using puppets for behavior rehearsal in social skills training sessions with young children." *Child Behavior Therapy* (in press).

LaGreca, A. M. and Santogross, D. A. "Social skills training with elementary school students: A behavioral group approach." *Journal of Consulting and Clinical Psychology* 48 (1980):220–227.

Oden, S. and Asher, S. R. "Coaching children in social skills for friendship making." *Child Development* 48 (1977):495–506.

CHAPTER 10

American Psychological Association, 1200 17th Street NW, Washington, D.C. 20036. (Information available on selecting a psychologist.)

Association for the Advancement of Behavior Therapy, 420 Lexington Avenue, New York, N.Y. 10170. (Information available on selecting a behavior therapist.)

Index

Doctors, fear of, 114
  overcoming, 131–136
Drabman, Ronald, 112

EEGs, 8
Emotional trauma, behavior
  problems and, 6–7
Enjoyable activities, use of, to
  reward children, 22–25
Epilepsy, 190
Experience(s)
  fears stemming from direct,
    115
  of others, fears based on,
    115–116

Fears, children's, 9, 114
  incorrect approaches for
    reducing, 118–120
  Progressive Exposure for
    reducing, 120–136
  reasons for development of,
    115–117
  *see also names of individual
    fears*
Fighting, 59–61
Florida, University of, 134
Friend-Making Game, 177–
  180

Genetic factors, personalities
  of parents and children
  and, 6
Giebenhain, Jean, 121
Good-Behavior Game, 88, 89–
  91, 93

Hospitals, fear of, 114, 120
  overcoming, 131–136
Hyperactive children, 190

Individuality, children's, 143–
  149

Learning from experience,
  behavior patterns and, 10,
  11

Medication, 189–191
Melamed, Barbara, 134
Misbehavior
  ignoring minor, 47–52
  reducing, by rewarding good
    behavior, 47, 59–62
Mississippi, University of, 121
  Medical Center, 112
Models, modeling, 63–64
  and effects of televised
    violence, 67–69
  to help children make
    friends, 177–180
  parents as, for children, 64–
    67
  as positive teaching
    approach, 69–75
  to teach alternatives to
    tantrums, 81–82

New situations, fear of, 116–
  117
Nightmares, 116
Noncompliance, 76–78
  how to handle, 87–94

O'Dell, Stan, 121

Parents Without Partners, 175
Perfection, avoiding unreal
  expectations of, 144–146
Personality, development of,
  over time, 8
Phobias, 118
Phrenology, 5
Praise, 17
  consistent, specific, and
    genuine, 20–22
  to strengthen child's good
    behavior, 18–20, 30–31